Complete Studio Tips

for Artists & Graphic Designers

Bill Gray

Revised by Paul Shaw

W. W. Norton & Company
New York · London

A NORTON PROFESSIONAL BOOK

For information about permission to reproduce selections from this book, write to
Permissions, W.W. Norton & Company, Inc., 500 Fifth Avenue, New York NY 10110

Manufacturing by Courier Westford

Library of Congress Cataloging-in-Publication Data

Gray, Bill, 1913 Sept. 28 –
    Complete studio tips for artists and graphic designers / Bill Gray. — Rev. / by Paul Shaw.
        p.   cm.
    Rev. ed. of: Studio Tips for artists & graphic designers, 1976; More studio tips
for artists and graphic designers, 1978
    "A Norton professional book" —
    Includes index
    ISBN 0-393-73000-X (pbk.)
    1. Graphic arts – Technique. I. Gray, Bill, 1913 Sept. 28 –
Studio tips for artists & graphic designers. II. Gray, Bill, 1913 Sept. 28 –
More studio tips for artists and graphic designers. III. Title.
    NC845. G73   1996
    702 .8 – de20   95 – 38579
                                                                    CIP

ISBN 0-393-73000-X (pbk.)

W.W. Norton & Company, Inc., 500 Fifth Avenue, New York NY 10110

W.W. Norton & Company Ltd., 10 Coptic Street, London WC1A 1PU

0 9 8 7 6 5 4 3 2 1

Contents

Preface to the Revised Edition

Bill Gray wrote Studio Tips, the first in the Tips series, in 1976, at a point midway between the demise of letterpress printing and metal type and the emergence of digital type and production. Much of his knowledge reflected the craft nature of the graphic design and commercial art world, a world where books were no substitute for accumulated real-life experience. Gray distilled fifty years of that experience into this book.

In the intervening period the digital revolution has made many of these practices seem obsolete. Yet, there are still many who are not fully digital in their work, and there are many occasions when digital sources and equipment are unavailable, unsuitable or unafford-able for a given task. Traditional tips still have a use-ful place on the bookshelf of every designer, student, and hobbyist. You will not find here the high-tech, whiz-bang tips that accompany computer software, but inexpensive, easy, and quick solutions to many of the commonplace yet nagging problems of daily design.

The revisions include not only obvious errors, but also some deletions and additions. Antiquated procedures and materials that are difficult to obtain today or no longer exist have been dropped, though letterpress and metal type information remains because of its underlying importance to understanding type. Some information on new products and technology has been added without going into depth about digital design. This is a subject for another book.

Organization
Some tips on organizing your work area

Economy of motion is important to every graphic artist. One way to save time and motion is to keep the things you are working with close to each other and conveniently close to you as you work. If you are using paint or ink and must prepare your brush and later clean it in water, keep your brushes, paint, spread pad, and water supply relatively close together and to the right of your work (if you are right-handed). You invite disastrous results if you have to carry a brush back and forth across your drawing — the paint may dry or you may knock something over or you may drip paint on your work.

Before you leave your work area at night raise your T-square high on the drawing board so that one end of the head does not protrude and "hold it" there with a pushpin. The cleaning person will not hit the head, possibly knocking some materials to the floor.

How to check the trueness of your drawing board and triangles

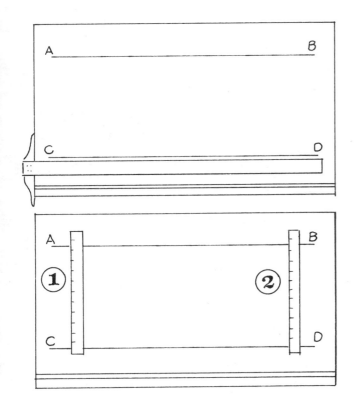

With your Tsquare head snug against the left edge of the drawing board, draw line AB, then line CD, relatively far apart.

Remove the Tsquare. Carefully measure the distance at left ①, and distance at right ②, between the two parallel lines. They should be exactly the same distance. If they are, your Tsquare and drawing board are "en rapport."

Holding the Tsquare snugly against the left edge of the drawing board, and with your triangle in the un-normal position, draw line AB. Flip the triangle to its normal position (dotted lines) and draw line AB. The two lines should be exactly the same line. Check all sides of all triangles in a similar manner.

How to make a "clothesline" file

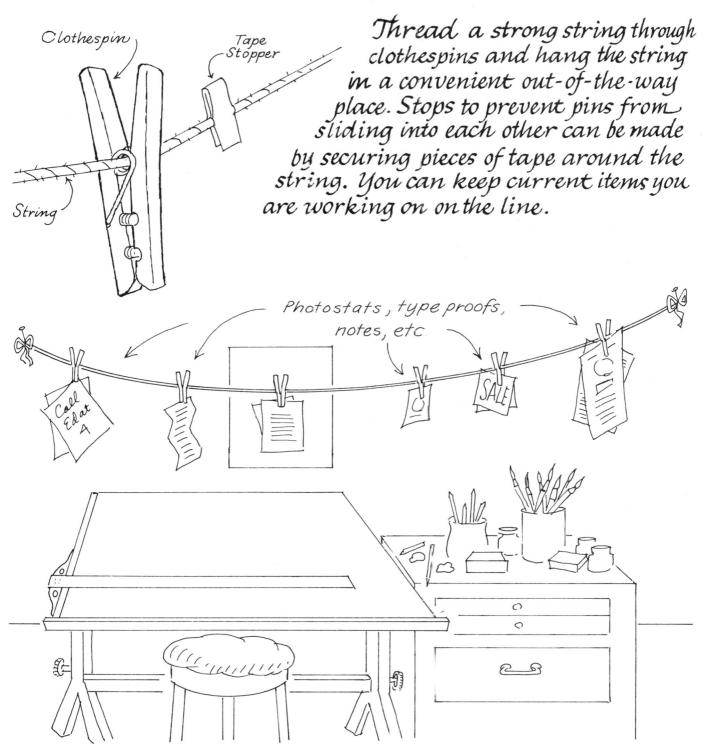

Clothespin

Tape Stopper

String

Thread a strong string through clothespins and hang the string in a convenient out-of-the-way place. Stops to prevent pins from sliding into each other can be made by securing pieces of tape around the string. You can keep current items you are working on on the line.

Photostats, type proofs, notes, etc.

Call Ed at 4

SALE

How to prevent stacked pieces from sliding

First cut a stiff card and fold as shown.

7" APPROX.

3"

Shape a "stopper" and secure to table top or floor with tape or pins.

Use on table or other top.

A small block of wood could be nailed or glued to the floor for a more permanent "stopper."

Many cards, boards, and other objects can be leaned against the wall and will not slide to the floor with this expedient temporary method.

How to make your drawing table, chair, and other furniture pieces slide more easily

If you have trouble moving your drawing board and other studio furniture...

Furniture slides

...buy some furniture slides (at any hardware store) and, turning the furniture upside down, nail the slides into the bottom legs. The furniture will then slide much more easily.

Bottom of Chair leg

How a slot cut in your drawing board can help in stripping pieces together

If you have many occasions to strip pieces together in a long continuous strip, a small slot cut in your drawing board may do the job. The slot to the left of your board allows paper strip to slide to the left and down without interfering with the action of your T-square. The hole can be cut with a sharp mat knife or a small pointed saw. The hole should be conveniently positioned on the drawing board so as not to interfere with normal work when not in use.

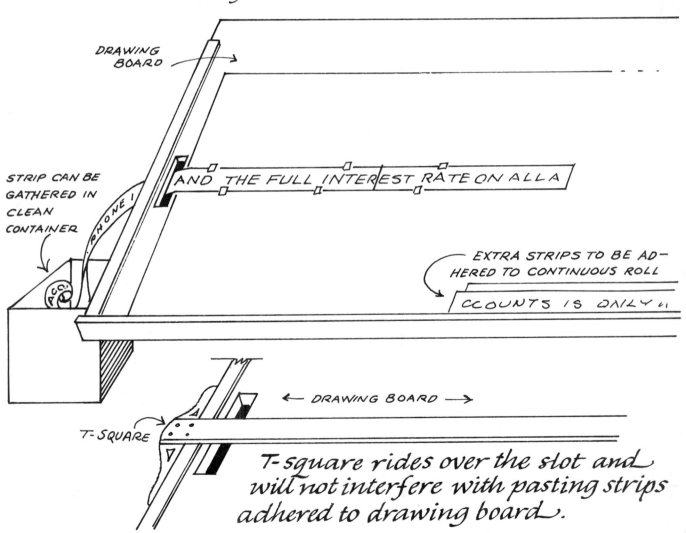

DRAWING BOARD

STRIP CAN BE GATHERED IN CLEAN CONTAINER

PHONE I

ACC.

AND THE FULL INTEREST RATE ON ALL A

EXTRA STRIPS TO BE AD-HERED TO CONTINUOUS ROLL

CCOUNTS IS DAILY ...

← DRAWING BOARD →

T-SQUARE

T-square rides over the slot and will not interfere with pasting strips adhered to drawing board.

How to draw an aligning line on your drawing board

If you do a lot of work on your drawing board with tissue and vellum sheets, it is a big help to have an aligning line or lines drawn on the surface of your board.

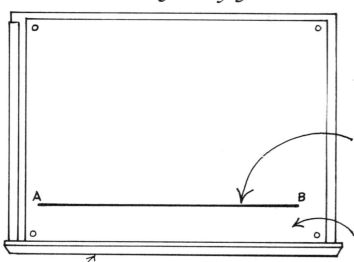

Attach a white card to your drawing board. This is the working surface of the drawing board. To help alignment, draw an aligning line (AB) in a convenient place to help you align translucent items.

WORKING SURFACE OF BOARD
(REPLACEABLE WHITE CARD)

DRAWING BOARD

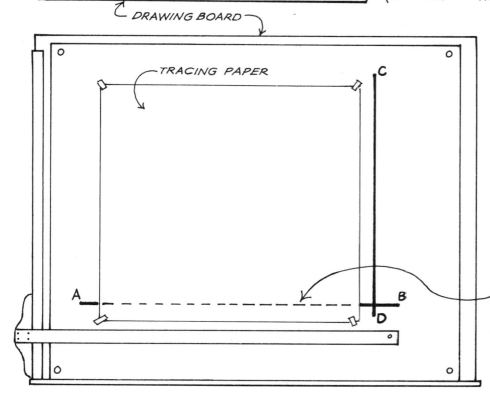

TRACING PAPER

Other aligning lines can be drawn (CD), but don't draw too many — it will be too confusing.

The lines are also an aid for aligning cards or illustration boards. The dotted line shows the aligning line under the tracing paper.

How to draw guide lines on your drawing board for checking and drawing rectangles

Most artists attach a thin white card or illustration board to their drawing board as a working surface that can be changed from time to time.

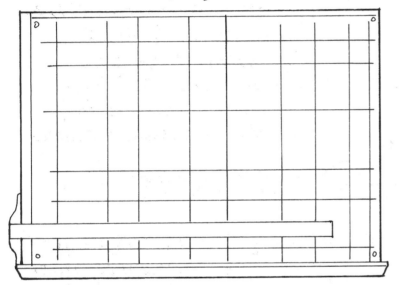

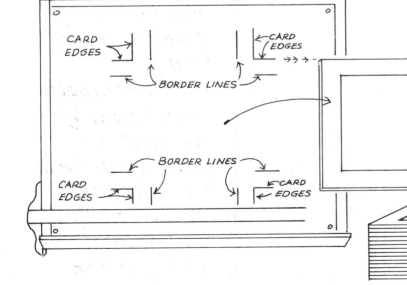

CARD EDGES

CARD EDGES

BORDER LINES

BORDER LINES

CARD EDGES

CARD EDGES

Thin ink lines forming rectangles of various sizes can be measured and marked unobtrusively on the card or board and used to check rectangles of layouts and the trueness or the "squareness" of photographs and other art.

If you have many cards of the same size on which borders are to be drawn, all exactly the same distance from the cards' edges, first draw corresponding marks on a clean drawing surface. Tape the cards, matching the marks, and rule in the borders with a pencil or pen. Remove the card and tape the next one and repeat the same method. This way will save time because no ruler is needed for measuring.

How to make a guide for slanted parallel elements

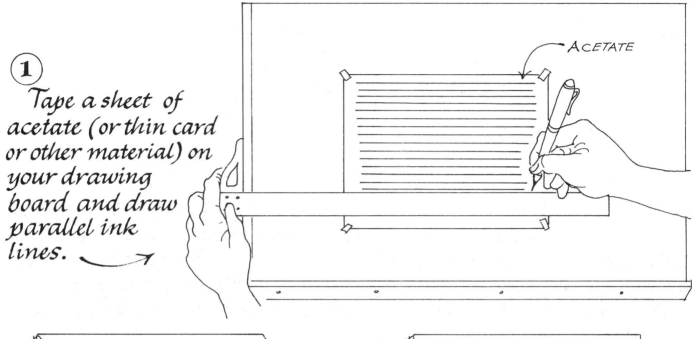

① Tape a sheet of acetate (or thin card or other material) on your drawing board and draw parallel ink lines. ⟶

ACETATE

② Slip the acetate guide under the tracing paper at the desired angle. Tape the guide so that it will not move.

Timothy

③ Following the parallel lines under the tracing paper, develop your design, as with the lettering above.

How to draw over the edge of your drawing board

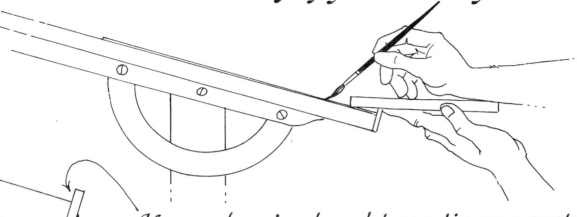

If your drawing board has a lip or a protruding edge at its lower side, it may be uncomfortable to draw near this edge. If you have this difficulty hold a thin board over the edge as a hand rest; a small tracing pad or other flat object may do.

There may be other situations where the use of a small flat piece as a hand rest can be helpful.

How to prevent ink or any other bottles from tipping over

← Cut a strip of paper about 6" x 1".

Cut a slit in the paper, as shown.

Where the neck of the bottle appears cut a small opening. Attach the paper strip to your drawing board with pins or tape.

The assembly can be attached to a small heavy card and moved.

CAN BE USED ON ALL TYPES OF BOTTLES.

INK

How to extend your layout area

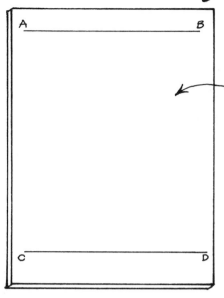

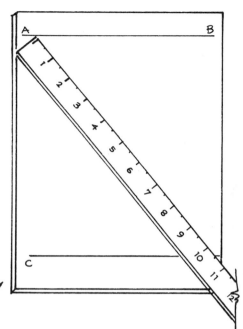

Suppose you have a layout problem. You want to divide the area between lines AB and CD into 26 equal parts. You decide to use the scale method, rotating your ruler until 26 units match points on the 2 lines. You find that a ruler will not fit.

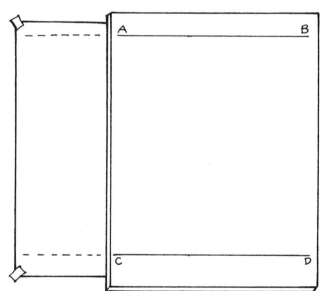

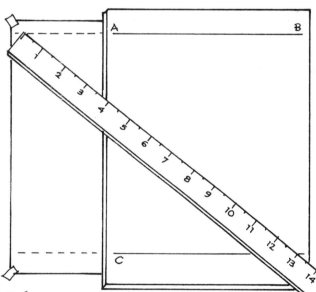

Insert a piece of paper larger than the distance between AB and CD, and extend the lines as shown with dotted lines above. Secure this paper so that it doesn't move as you proceed.

You can now conveniently mark off 26 equal parts (½" each), draw the lines, and proceed with your layout. Extension paper can be discarded.

How to keep your layout pad and tissue sheets from moving

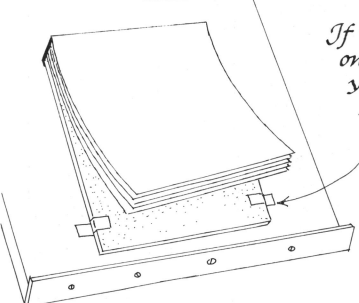

If your layout pad moves on the drawing board as you draw on it, attach small strips of tape to the pad backing and to the board.

If the tissue sheets of the pad move ...

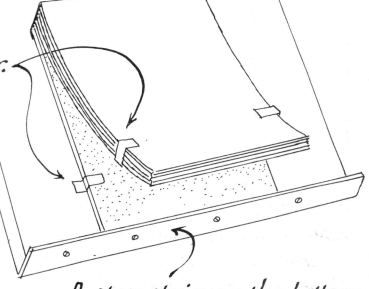

... attach strips of tape around all of the sheets to bind them all together. As you need new sheets to work on, pick the tape from the top sheet with a fingernail, lift and remove the sheet you have just worked on, then re-attach the tape.

A stop strip on the bottom of the drawing board is great for resting the pad against.

How to position art on the drawing board

Art, or a mechanical paste-up, should be positioned toward the left side of your drawing board and should be close to the head of your T square as shown

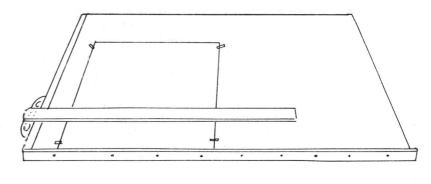

here. In this way there will be less of a chance for making errors since you will be able to control your T square much more easily and lines that you draw with the T square and triangles will be much more accurate.

How to prevent things from sliding off the drawing board

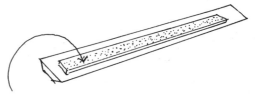

A large piece of sandpaper can be rubber cemented to the right side of your drawing board, as shown, to prevent tools and other objects from sliding down the board and falling on the floor.

Attach a thin strip to the bottom of the drawing board. Jars, pencils, brushes, etc., will then not slide off the board onto the floor. It is also great for resting art work against when erasing.

Glue strips of sandpaper on bottoms of bottles, rulers, and other things that slide easily.

13

How to prevent objects from sliding on your board

Did you ever have the questionable
thrill of having a large jar of paint
slide down your drawing board?
To prevent this from happening,
paint rubber cement on the bottoms
of any objects that may slide.

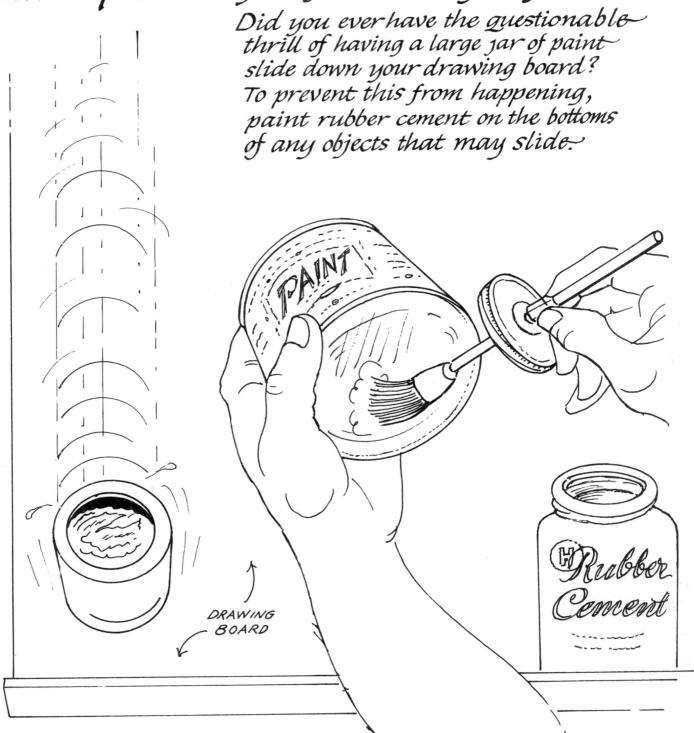

DRAWING
BOARD

PAINT

Rubber Cement

How to prevent knocking things off the board with your T square

If you are one of those artists (I am) who sometimes works with a cluttered drawing board and you are constantly knocking items to the floor, draw a heavy line at the extreme limits of your T square and to the right of your working area. This line acts as a boundary. Never put any items to the left of it, where they would interfere with the action of your T square or get knocked down.

How always to have a pen wiper and wipe rag handy

A piece of cheesecloth can be hung at each end of your drawing board so that the cloth can be used conveniently at either side for wiping pens, pointed pencils, or other tools. The cheesecloth pieces can be washed daily — or whenever necessary. Washed cheesecloth is more absorbent than most other rag material. Wring the rags out at the sink and they will dry while hanging.

How to make an inexpensive portable "light table"

Buy a piece of heavy plate glass (18" x 24") from the local glazier. Have him smooth the edges. Then tape the edges well with adhesive or any other tape. Resting this glass on your lap and a table edge, place a small lamp on the floor beneath the glass and use the glass as a light box. Flashlights or other battery lamps can also be used. To prevent eye strain, you can frost the glass, or have it done by a glazier.

Glass

Tips on working with a lightbox

If you need guidelines for your lettering, but don't want them to show, you can draw them on the <u>back</u> of your paper or bristol board. Then, with a lightbox, write on the <u>front</u>.

Use a lightbox for certificate "fill-ins." Draw guidelines with character count markings on a blank sheet of paper. Place underneath certificates.

A window (during daylight) can be used as a "lightbox" if necessary. This is good for tracing large pictures.

16

How to use a metal T-square

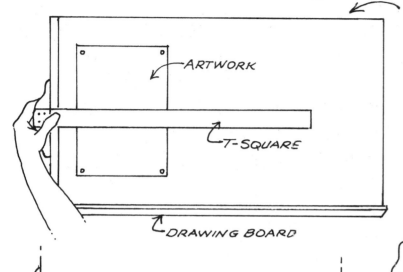

ARTWORK

T-SQUARE

DRAWING BOARD

Always keep work to the left of your drawing board near the head of your T-square. Hold the head of the T-square with your left hand (if you are right-handed). It can be moved easily in this manner.

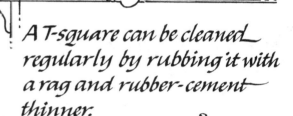

A T-square can be cleaned regularly by rubbing it with a rag and rubber-cement thinner.

To check a T-square, draw a straight line, turn it upside down, and check the top to see that you draw the exact same line with the same edge.

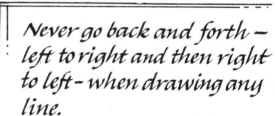

Never go back and forth — left to right and then right to left — when drawing any line.

Never use the bottom edge of a T-square to draw straight lines, especially ink lines.

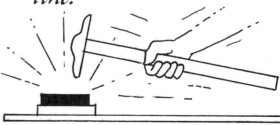

<u>Never</u> use T-square as a hammer.

How to prevent ink from spreading under tools

If you have trouble with ink spreading under your ruler, triangles, and T square when you use a ruling pen or other pens, adhere pieces of tape under the edge that you use. You can laminate several layers on top of one another if necessary. This lifts the tool away from the drawing surface and will *prevent* the ink from smudging the art work.

Triangle

Tape

Tape

T square

Ruler

How to use paste wax to help tools slide

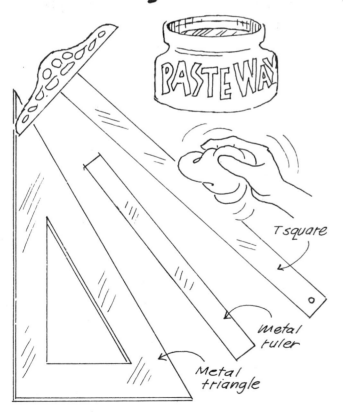

PASTE WAX

T square

Metal ruler

Metal triangle

If you want your tools to slide more easily, rub a light amount of paste wax on the under side and they will move easily over your drawing and board. Do not apply too much wax or it will have the opposite effect – make the tools sticky. Waxing is especially good for metal tools, but it may work on other materials. Sometimes a little wax on the sliding parts of a file drawer help the drawer slide more easily.

How to use a metal T-square to cut very long cards

Line up the metal top edge of the T-square with the line to be cut on the card. Insert 2 push pins, one at either end of the T-square, so that it will not move as you cut the card with a knife. If the card is very thick make the cut in two passes: create a groove, then more finish the cut.

once lightly to deeply to

Line of cut

Card to be cut

A long metal bar can also be used in the same manner as above.

✳ Never use a plastic or wood T-square to cut against.

Use a sharp mat knife to cut the cardboard.

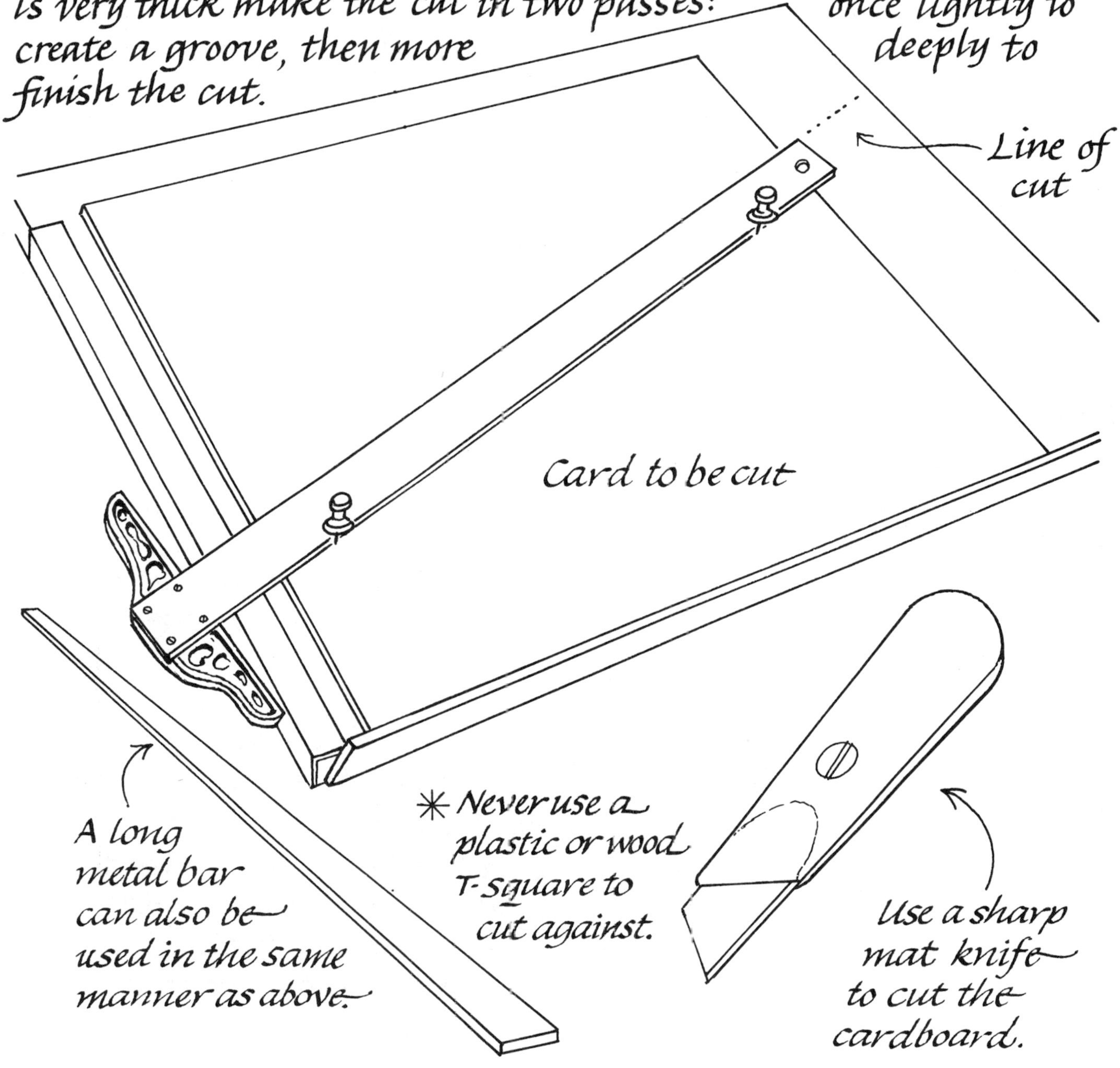

How to use a paper's edge to check alignment

The straight long edge of a sheet of letter paper can be used to check alignment of elements on a layout.

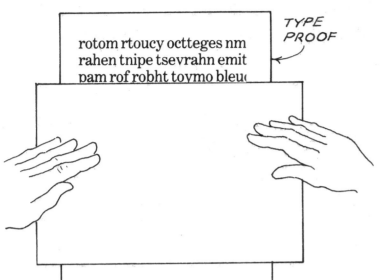

TYPE PROOF

rotom rtoucy octteges nm
rahen tnipe tsevrahn emit
pam rof robht toymo bleud

① The straight edge can be moved to check alignment of all the lines on a type proof.

② It can also be used to check alignment of elements already pasted down on a layout (or mechanical) that cannot be checked with a T-square.

LAYOUT

PARK ZIPS METS

PHILLIES ACE NO-HITS N.Y. LEADERS

IT'S A HIT IN ANY LEAGUE

ZIPPY'S

GOOD FOR WHAT ALES YOU!

ACETATE

③ A piece of acetate with a thin, straight black line drawn on it can also be used to check alignment. It has an advantage over the paper — it is transparent, allowing you to see all the other elements on the layout.

How to get unusual effects with felt-nib pens

You can get unusual textural and linear effects with felt-nib pens by splitting the ends and separating the splits.

STENCIL KNIFE

MARKER OR
WIDE FELT-NIB PEN

PENCIL
FELT NIB
PEN

DOUBLE VISION

Pre-split felt-tip and metal poster pens are available in several combinations of stripes.

Grasses, trees, etc., can be drawn with interesting treatment and thin ink lines added.

All kinds of textural effects are possible. Using different colors of felt-nib pens together gives still more possibilities.

How to use a toothbrush or atomizer for spray effects

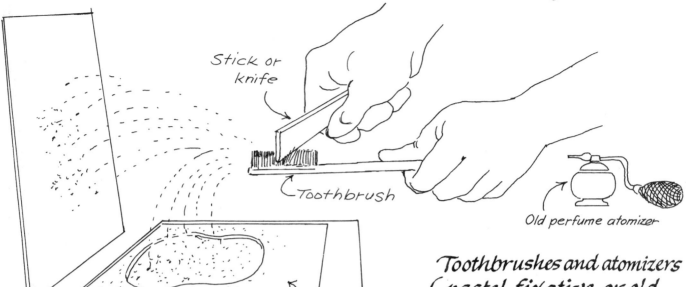

Stick or knife

Toothbrush

Old perfume atomizer

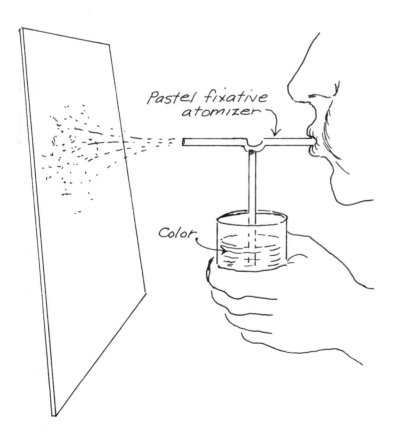

mask

Pastel fixative atomizer

Color

Toothbrushes and atomizers (pastel fixative or old perfume dispenser) can both be used as effective spraying devices. At left, use of the toothbrush is shown. Dip the brush in paint and use a knife or small stick to spatter the art.

Next, the use of an atomizer with thin color (ink, watercolor, and other media) to achieve spray effects is shown.

Practice with different solutions.

How to prevent smudged ink lines

If you are a careful, neat worker, you will probably have no trouble with wet ink lines when you use a T-square. If you are not, try some of the hints below to keep your drawing or mechanical clean and neat.

① The dash line above represents the pencil line you want to ink in on your mechanical.

② Place a long, thin strip of cardboard near this line but not covering it.

③ Carefully place your T-square over this strip, line up the line, and ink it in. The strip underneath is indicated by the dotted line.

CROSS SECTION OF ③ ABOVE

T-SQUARE
STRIP
MECHANICAL

← DRAWING BOARD →

* NOTE
YOU CAN TURN THE T-SQUARE OVER AND CEMENT A LONG STRIP OF BLOTTING PAPER NEAR (¼") THE INKING EDGE. STRIPS CAN ALSO BE GLUED TO OTHER TOOLS.

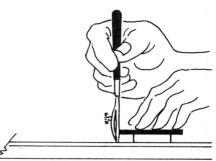

The diagram above shows the position of the inking tool—vertically or at a 90° angle from the drawing surface.

This is the kind of line you will get if you press the ruling pen too hard against the T-square.

This is the line you will get if pen slopes away from drawing surface or is not at a 90° angle.

How to steady your drawing hand when retouching

An aid to your drawing hand in sketching in fine lines in ink or in retouching lettering, etc. is your other hand, as shown below.

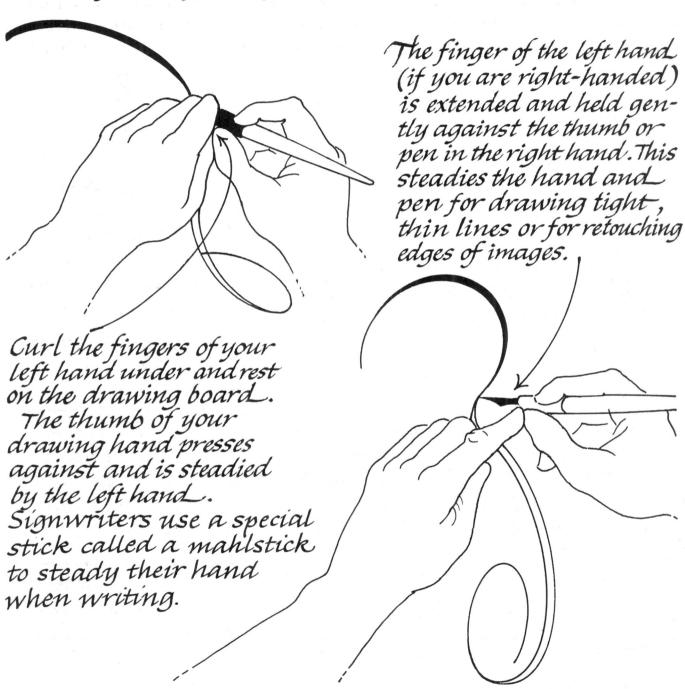

The finger of the left hand (if you are right-handed) is extended and held gently against the thumb or pen in the right hand. This steadies the hand and pen for drawing tight, thin lines or for retouching edges of images.

Curl the fingers of your left hand under and rest on the drawing board. The thumb of your drawing hand presses against and is steadied by the left hand. Signwriters use a special stick called a mahlstick to steady their hand when writing.

How to erase

The most important thing to keep in mind when erasing is that you want to remove the spot completely — with the least possible damage if any to the surface of your drawing. After choosing the correct eraser, rub the spot gently in the actions shown below. Do not attack the surface roughly. The arrows show the directions in which the eraser moves. One should erase in many different directions, not just one.

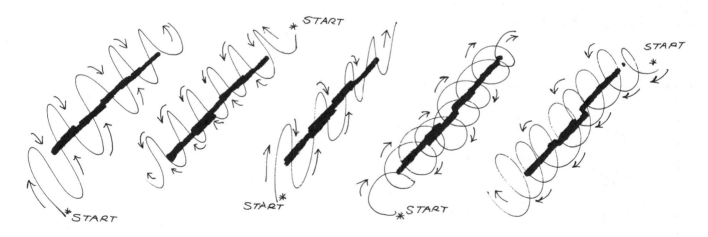

As you erase, blow the crumbs away. Otherwise you may grind dirty particles back into the surface.

The diagrams show successive directions and the movement of the eraser and hand.

How to use an electric-drill sander as an eraser

Suppose you wanted to remove a section of a painted billboard, or a large painted name sign over a storefront, or a painted name on a directory in a public building or elsewhere. An electric drill with a sander attachment can be used to "erase" the unwanted part.

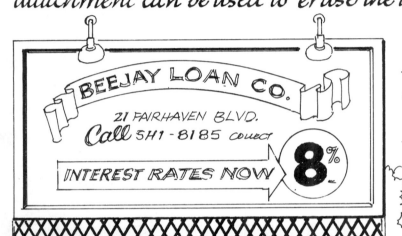

Just sand the unwanted area out carefully, clean it well, and repaint the new information as shown above and at left. A little retouching may be necessary.

Ways to get a deckle-edge effect on paper

Shown below are 5 different ways of creating a deckle-edge effect on paper.

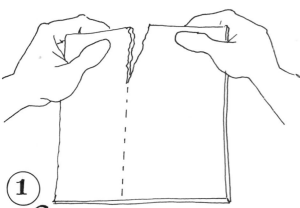

① Carefully tear paper along a folded line. If the paper is heavy wet it first with an eyedropper.

② Hold a saw firmly against the edge and tear the paper, pulling against the saw.

③ With scissors, cut back and forth along a line.

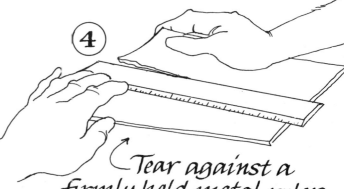

Tear against a firmly held metal ruler or straightedge.

⑤ Burn, here and there, and clean up. This gives the deckle edge an antique look as well.

How to use an aerosol spray can

First carefully read all of the instructions and directions on the can. Some of these are repeated here for emphasis.

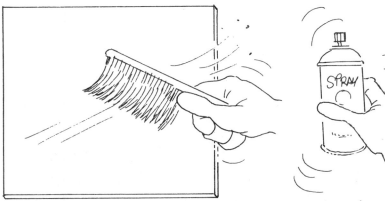

Be sure the surface to be sprayed is clean.

Shake the can well before use.

Test the spray on scrap to be sure it works well.

Always keep the top on when not in use.

Use a needlepoint to reopen if the spray hole gets jammed.

A light spray will waterproof paper cups.

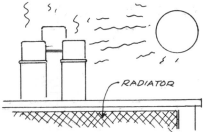

Never store cans on a heated surface — they may burst.

Use a moist hanky when using spray a great deal.

If you must remove spray fixative from art, try some lacquer thinner and a rag or a cotton ball – carefully.

How to use fixative to prevent tape from pulling up the surface of your working card

If you use a card cover on your drawing board as a working surface, you will find that when you remove art work which has been <u>taped</u> down, the tape will leave scuff marks.

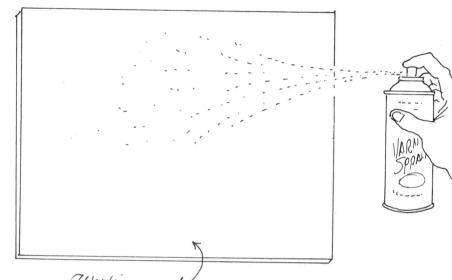

Working card

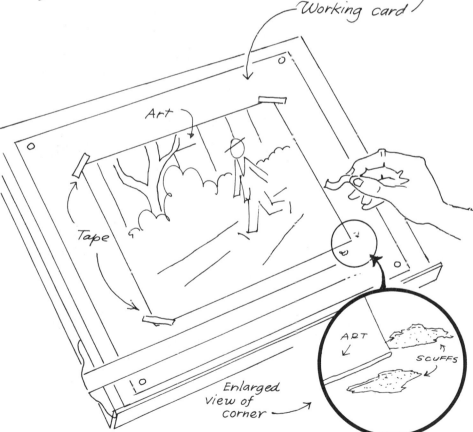

Art

Tape

Enlarged view of corner

ART

SCUFFS

To avoid this, spray the card cover first with acrylic spray coating fixative; then when you pick up the tape, it will not tear the surface.

As you change cover cards from time to time, spray them generously as shown above so that this (see circle) will not happen to your cover.

How to remove tape used to secure art to a board

Whenever tape is used to hold art down on the drawing board or anywhere else, ALWAYS remove it from the inside, or art part, to the outside. NEVER pull tape in towards the art to remove it. If art is on the board you may remove part of a ply (the art side) if you pull the tape toward the art, with disastrous results.

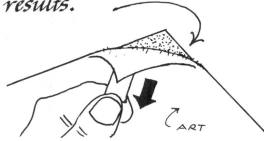

ART

How to correct a black ink line on a white background

If you make a mistake drawing black line art on white illustration board, here is one way to correct it

GRAPFIC

The above lettering was misspelled and the F must be painted out with white paint and changed to an H.

GRAPHIC

GRAPHIC

The retouched area is sprayed with fixative. This step can be repeated

GRAPHIC

Now paint the new letter.

How a soda straw can be used to transfer liquid from one container to another

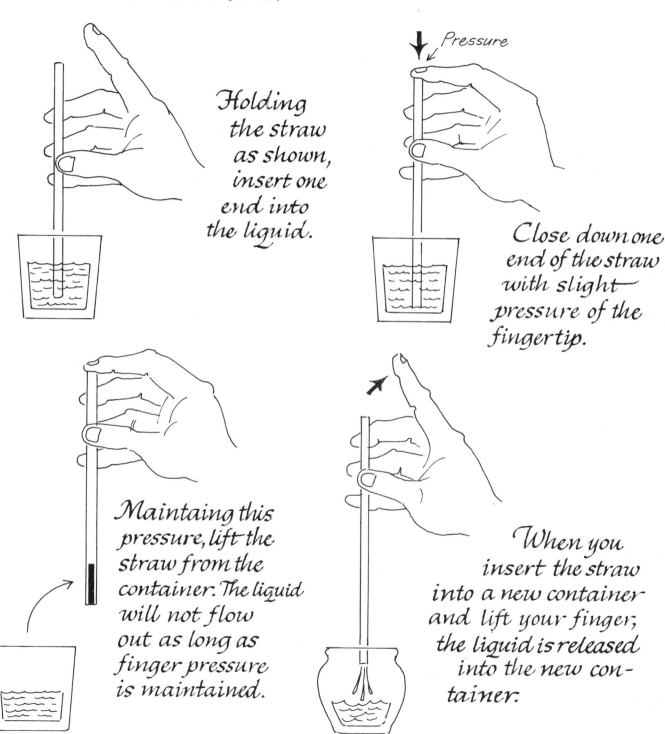

Holding the straw as shown, insert one end into the liquid.

Pressure

Close down one end of the straw with slight pressure of the fingertip.

Maintaing this pressure, lift the straw from the container. The liquid will not flow out as long as finger pressure is maintained.

When you insert the straw into a new container and lift your finger; the liquid is released into the new container.

How to make a template for repeated patterns

If you have to draw many duplicate designs — such as lettering signs — cut a template as shown.

Knife

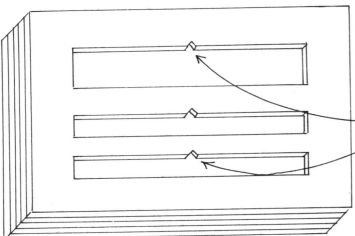

First make your layout and cut out rectangles for guide lines on all copies.

Nicks can be cut in the slots to show the center line.

Using the same procedure, you can make templates for all sorts of other designs.

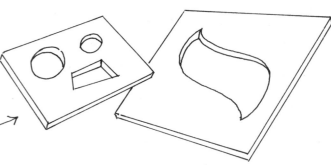

32

Simple ways to draw on the side of a container

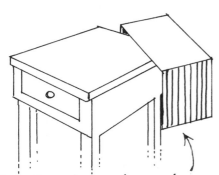

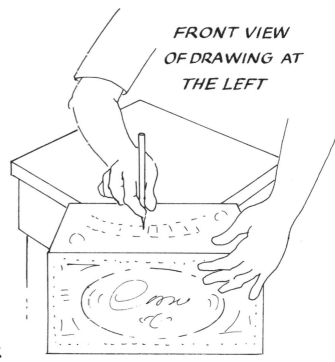

FRONT VIEW
OF DRAWING AT
THE LEFT

Box is placed on the corner of a table. The right hand rests on the table top. The left hand holds the box against the table corner.

Use a large or small table, depending on what works best.

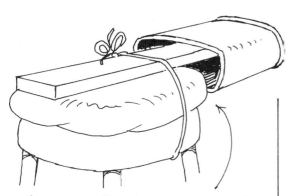

The corner of a large flat book on top of a round chair seat holds the box. This is the same principle that is shown in the illustration above.

A long flat stick is tied to a chair top and used as an arm rest. Container is placed over the stick and held while being worked on.

Pile books around a square or round box. A small flat book is used as an arm or hand rest.

How to butt 2 pieces in an irregular joint

Suppose that you want to join two pieces of coloraid paper together in an irregular joint.

To begin with, rubber cement or paste down the first color on a board. ⟶

Mark the irregular joint before pasting the second color to the first color.

Carefully cut the joint through both papers, removing the unwanted part of the second color.

Carefully lift the second color sheet and remove the unwanted part of the first sheet so that lumps will not show. Reset the second color, and you should have a perfect mortise. ⟶

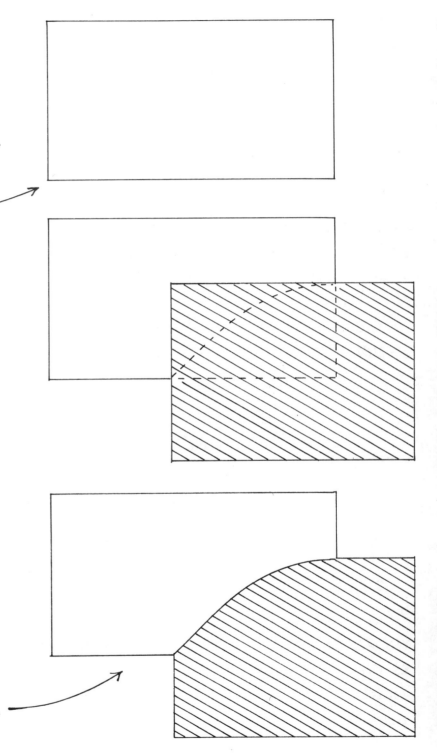

Leftovers
How to make expensive-looking boards from cheap cards

You can laminate colored papers (coloraid, textured, gift-wrap papers, etc.) onto the backs of cheap cardboards, such as the backs of sketching pads, to get expensive-looking boards.

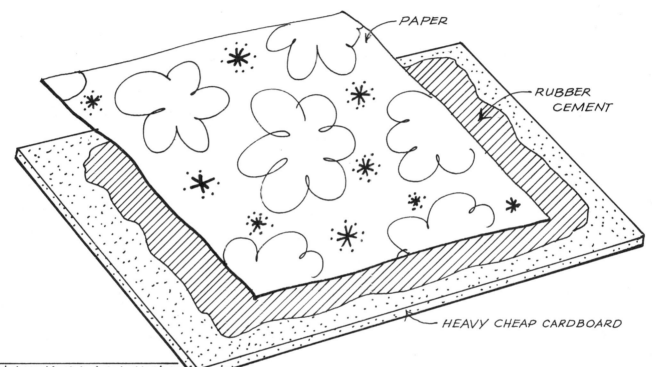

PAPER

RUBBER CEMENT

HEAVY CHEAP CARDBOARD

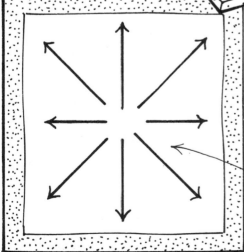

Paper is dry-mounted onto the card. Slip sheets can be used. Pressure with the soft back of your hand is better than a celluloid triangle (or similar hard tool). A protective sheet of paper should cover the paper as you apply pressure from the center out to the edges.
Card can later be trimmed to a smaller size if desired.

How to use small scrap pieces of cards

① Scraping together spilled rubber cement and the like.

② Push pin holds card for paint spreader for preparing brush.

Call garage at 10 for oil change

Mail money to Stacey at school.

Get soda for party

③ Use for temporary notes and reminders. Card will fit into wallet with money.

TAPE

Jinnie Call Bill urgent! Patrice

④ Write notes for others (telephone messages, visitors, etc.).

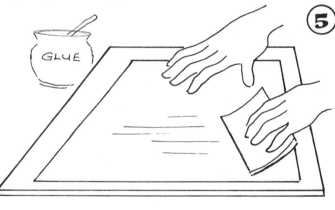

GLUE

⑤ They can be used as brayers for smoothing down large pasted areas.

PLEASE KEEP DOOR CLOSED

WET PAINT

WILL BE BACK AT 2 PM J.M.

⑥ Use for small temporary signs.

Save samples of different kinds of paper and board. Use to test inks, gouache, watercolors and felt-tip markers.

How to use tissue and vellum pad backs over again

Instead of discarding the backs of paper pads (tissue, vellum, bond, etc.) save them for possible uses as demonstrated below.

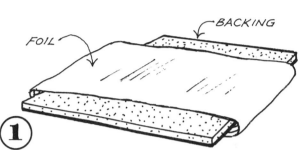

① Stretch aluminum foil around them and use for a disposable paint palette.

② Use for cutting templates or unusual patterns. Sandpaper the edges.

③ Laminate colored or patterned paper onto them for expensive-looking heavy boards.

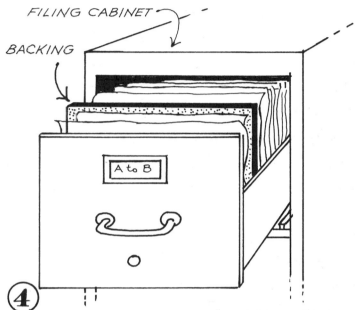

④ They can be used as "stiffeners" in floppy files. Insert them here and there so that papers don't collapse.

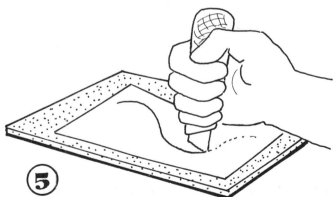

⑤ Use as a cutting-board backing to save your table tops and drawing boards.

Pencils
How to make selecting the right pencil easier.

If you use many grades of lead in mechanical pencils, it is a good idea to use one pencil for each grade of lead and mark the grade with a white tape on all sides of the pencil shaft, as shown. You will then never have difficulty picking up the right pencil grade.

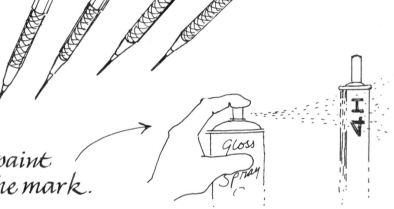

Another method is to mark the sides of the pencil with black or white paint and apply varnish spray to the mark.

How to speed up a pencil rendering

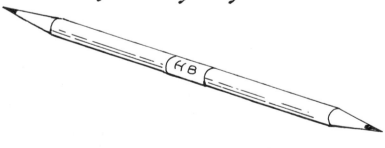

If you are using a wood-clenched pencil and are in a hurry to complete an assignment sharpen both ends of the pencil. This will save time; just switch around to the other end when one end becomes blunt. Mark the grade of the lead on a tape and attach to the center of the pencil. If you like, one end of the pencil can have a chisel edge, the other a point.

Information about pencils

| 9H | 8H | 7H | 6H | 5H | 4H | 3H | 2H | H | F | HB | B | 2B | 3B | 4B | 5B | 6B |

Pencils are graded from 9H (hardest) to 6B (softest). The lead is thinnest in hard pencils and large in soft.

You can save money by using a pencil extender for small pencils.
    The extender gives continued balance.

Extender

Pencil

Stabilo pencils come in many grades and colors and...

... are used for marking on glass, acetate, plastic, metal and glossy surfaces.

STABILO

Push release

Grip

Lead

Mechanical pencils are most economical. When needed, leads are easily replaced and can be purchased in all grades.

Automatic or "clicker" mechanical pencils have lead thicknesses of .1, .07, .05 and .03 mm.

"Clicker" button

Lead

The lead is advanced by "clicking" a button on the top or side of the pencil.

How to sharpen pencil *points*

The suggestions below are for pencil points on either wood-clinched or mechanical pencils.

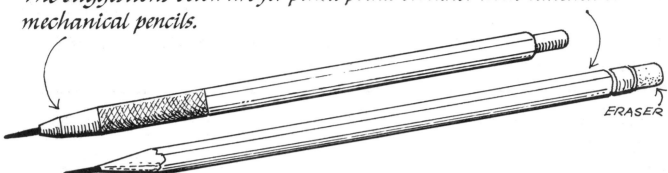

ERASER

There are 2 kinds of points that can be fashioned on a sandpaper or other pencil pointer —

CONICAL OR CHISEL

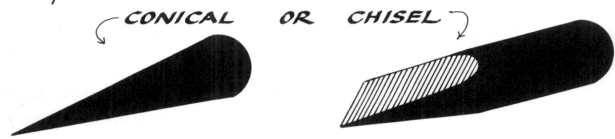

When drawing long lines with a conical point, keep rotating the pencil as you use it. The conical point is also used for lettering.

The flat or chisel edge is preferred by most designers for drawing long straight lines.

Suggestions

1. Keep your pencils sharp. The same is true for mechanical pencils. It's the point that counts.
2. Wipe the lead point after preparing it.
3. The proper grade of softness or hardness is important. You must inspect your writing surface to determine the grade to use.
4. Emery boards and nail files can also be used as pencil pointers.

How to make your own sandpaper pencil pointer

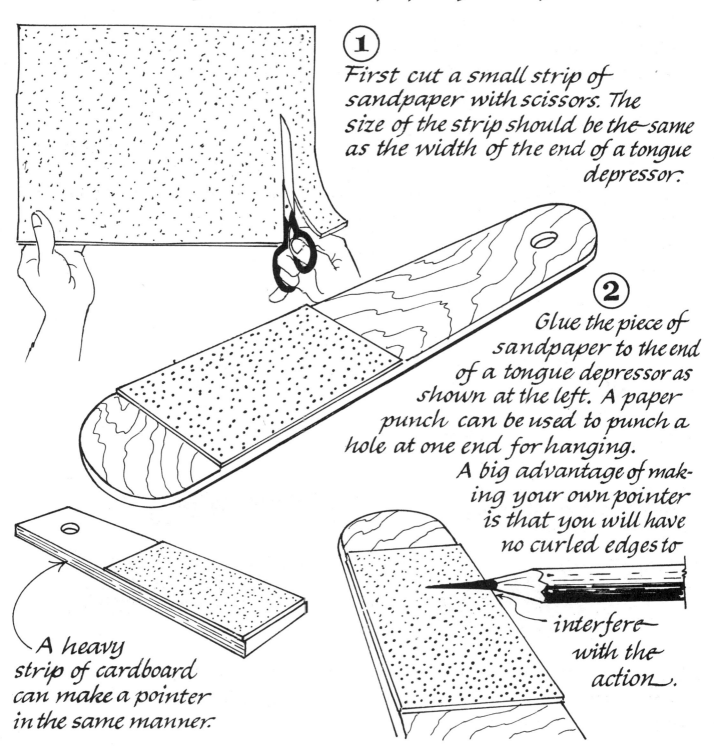

1 First cut a small strip of sandpaper with scissors. The size of the strip should be the same as the width of the end of a tongue depressor.

2 Glue the piece of sandpaper to the end of a tongue depressor as shown at the left. A paper punch can be used to punch a hole at one end for hanging.

A big advantage of making your own pointer is that you will have no curled edges to interfere with the action.

A heavy strip of cardboard can make a pointer in the same manner.

How to use a burnt cork for shading effects

If charcoal sticks or graphite pieces are not available and you need to achieve a soft shading effect, burned cork might serve your purpose. So save those corks from office parties, etc. The smudged area can be fixed with workable fixative when finished.

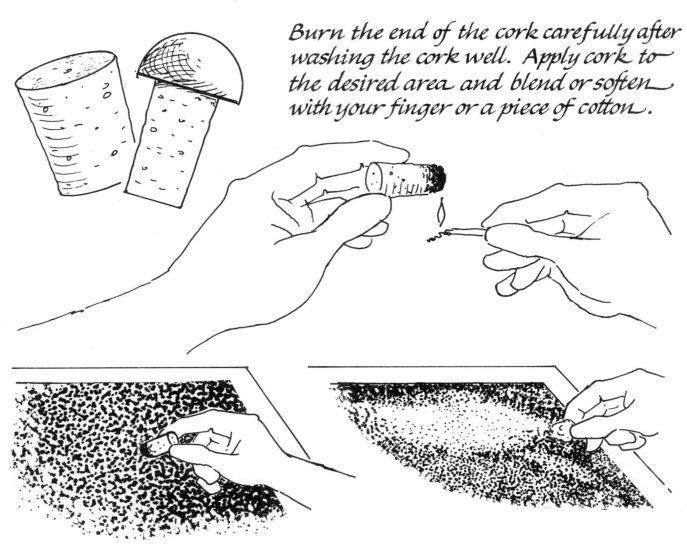

Burn the end of the cork carefully after washing the cork well. Apply cork to the desired area and blend or soften with your finger or a piece of cotton.

Clouds and rounded shapes on art already done can be reinforced with a soft charcoal tone effect. Kneaded erasers can be used to pick up highlights.

42

Kinds of erasers and their uses

 **Soft pliable** rubber eraser is an all purpose eraser that cleans as it erases. It is the most common one used.

 **Kneaded eraser** for pencil, chalk, pastel and charcoal. It can be shaped to any convenient form and is nonabrasive. It is gray in color.

 **Ink eraser** is hard and abrasive. It will scratch out stubborn ink marks.

 Art gum eraser is free of grease and cannot scratch. It crumbles. It is used to remove pencil marks from inked art.

 **Plastic** (VINYL) drafting eraser for use on tracing cloth, film, or paper. It is hard and does not crumble.

 Paper-wrapped erasers are pencil shaped, soft or abrasive. For use in very small areas and can be pointed.

 **Dry, clean pad** eraser comes in a mesh bag with gum bits that sift through. It is used to clean large jobs such as signs and charts.

 Fiber glass eraser is cigar-shaped. Has a fiber-glass brush tip and is used for extremely difficult erasures.

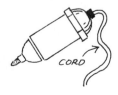 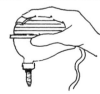 **Electric erasers** for general use. Move them gently in a rotating manner. Nibs are either soft or abrasive and are interchangeable.

Other kinds of "erasers"

Razor blades and knives can be used to remove heavy deposits of ink and paint. Use a gentle scraping motion. When you are near the surface of the paper, switch over to one of the other more conventional methods.

Cotton balls, Q-tips, swabs, and small pieces of clean rags can be used with rubber cement thinner to take grease, scuff marks, and other stubborn marks away. Use a gentle scrubbing action.

Erasing fluids (2 bottles — one a hypochlorite and the other an acid) can be applied successively on the mark and removed with a blotter.

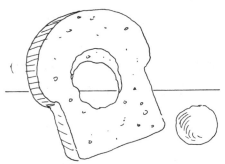

If there are no other erasers around, and you desperately need to erase some pencil smudges on a piece of art, take the center from a slice of any white wheat bread, roll it into a ball, and use it like you would an eraser. It really works.

Special abrasive powders are made for use in airbrushes for extremely difficult situations when all other erasing methods have failed.

How spraying minimizes marker bleeding and creeping

A

B

If you use marker felt-nib pens on porous or semiporous paper or cards for signs, charts, or other purposes, spray your working area first with fixative. This minimizes bleeding and creeping of forms into each other, especially if the lines are close together as in A to the left. Some bleeding and creeping may occur if you just spray with workable fixative first. For maximum effectiveness spray your working area generously with acrylic spray coating and when the area is dry, proceed with your work. The images you draw will now be clear-cut as in B compared to A.

Always test on scrap paper first.

How to make a fussy ball-point pen work

You can do something about a ball point pen not working, providing it has ink in it. Touch the tip of the pen to something hot (like a cigarette tip or a flame), and it will work. Also, a new tip sometimes has a coating on it which must be removed before the pen will work properly.

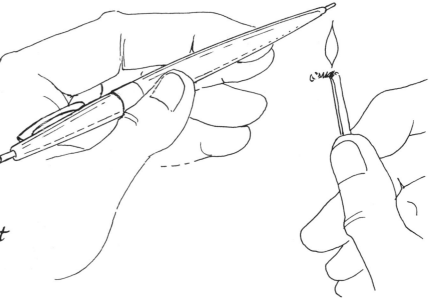

Tips on brushes

Mark one good brush (with white tape, e.g.) for use with white paint *only*. You will always have clean white strokes if you do this. *Never* use this brush with *any* color in it.

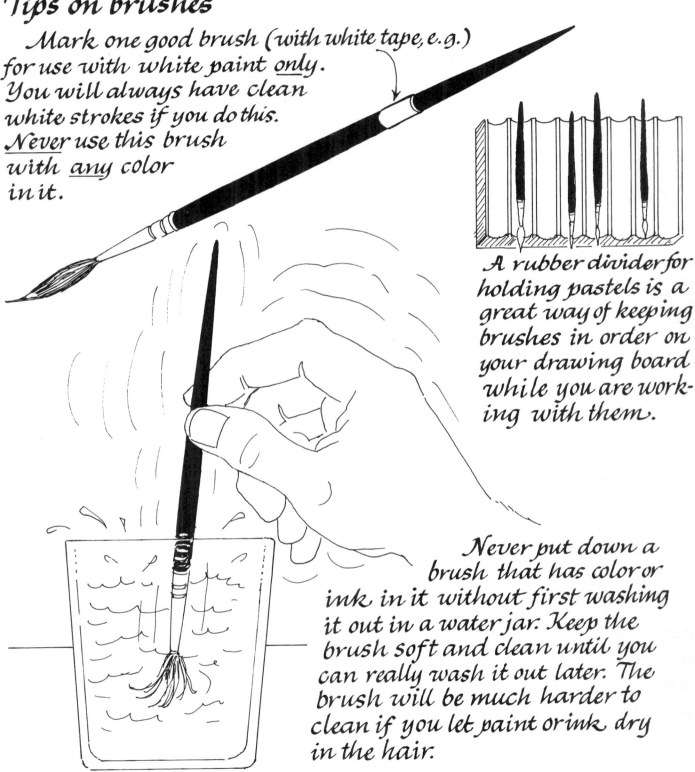

A rubber divider for holding pastels is a great way of keeping brushes in order on your drawing board while you are working with them.

Never put down a brush that has color or ink in it without first washing it out in a water jar. Keep the brush soft and clean until you can really wash it out later. The brush will be much harder to clean if you let paint or ink dry in the hair.

How to reshape an old turned brush

If you have an old neglected brush that you think could still be usable, even though it is split and turned, immerse it into a water-soluble glue or mucilage (5 and 10¢ store items).

Then work the hairs between your fingers and shape them. Continue this action until the brush is almost dry. The brush can then be hung and left suspended for a few days to dry. Or you can punch the brush's handle through a thin card and stand it in an empty glass or cup to dry. After a few days, wash the brush. By then it should have its normal manufactured shape back. If not, throw it away.

How to wash brushes used for acrylic painting

Brushes used in painting with acrylic resin paints can be easily cleaned with alcohol and soap and water.

① Dip brush in alcohol after removing all excess paint on a rag.

Alcohol

② Dip and swish around in mild soap and water

Mild Soap and Water

③ Dip for a few minutes into white vinegar.

WHITE VINEGAR

④ Wash thoroughly in water.

⑤ Shape with fingers when wet-dry and store away for next job.

How to store good brushes for a long period of time

You may take a long vacation or break your drawing arm (heaven forbid) and not use your good sable or other brushes as a result. Your brushes should be stored in this case with moth flakes or mothballs in one of the ways suggested below.

A clean old cigar box can hold most of the short brushes. Seal the lid with tape when closed.

All the containers should have either the moth flakes or mothballs generously distributed therein.
Use cardboard rollers from dispenser paper-towel rolls, etc. — a little wax paper for ends.
Mailing tubes are strong and have their own tops.

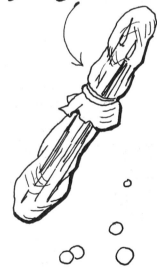

Take an extra plastic bag at the produce counter of the market. They are great for storing brushes of any size.

49

How to make two brush holders

Regular plastic soda straws can be cut in half and taped to the edge of your drawing board to hold brushes that you are working with.

Brush can easily be lifted from and inserted into straw.

This is an expedient method of holding brushes. More permanent storage would be in a jar.

Tape could be reinforced with push pins.

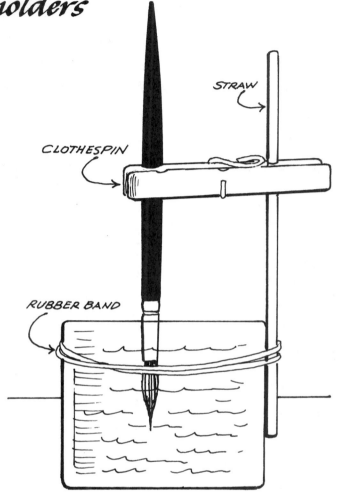

Brush can be suspended handily in water and held by a clothespin and drinking straw which are attached to each other. The straw, or a small flat stick, is held to the water glass with a rubber band. Glass should have flat sides.

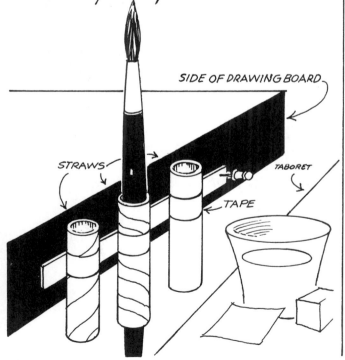

How to make a holder for delicate pens and knives

Save expensive cigar containers or ask someone who smokes them (cigars) to save the containers for you. Some toothbrushes are bought in similar cases. They come in glass, metal, or plastic. They are handy and safe for carrying stencil knives, technical pens, or other unguarded pens. Be sure that the container is long enough to accommodate the pen or knife. You may have other things you wish to store.

A small piece of sponge can be glued to the inside end of the top and kept moist for carrying technical pens, making them less apt to dry out and malfunction. These containers are good for storing on weekends and vacations

If it is a glass container wrap adhesive or other tape around it, in case it breaks accidentally. These containers can be easily carried around in a pocket or handbag.

How to make a carrier for brushes and pens

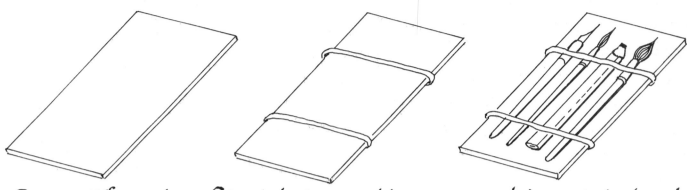

Cut a stiff card any convenient size, such as pocket size.

Stretch two rubber bands around the card – one at the top, one at the bottom –

and insert the brushes and pens under the rubber bands for carrying.

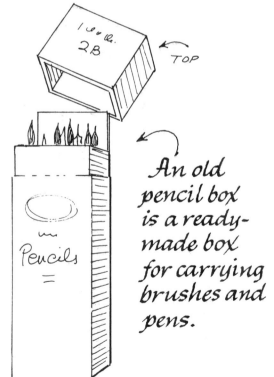

An old pencil box is a ready-made box for carrying brushes and pens.

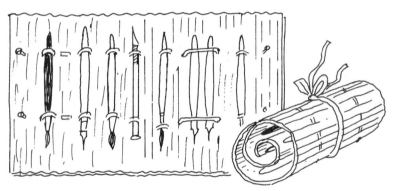

An old bamboo mat or an old place mat with brushes and pens neatly laid inside can be rolled and tied. A thread or rubber band can be laced in and out of the top and bottom of the mat to hold everything in place.

Drawing Instruments
Tips on the care and use of drawing instruments

Every graphic designer should have his own set of good drawing (or drafting) instruments. He should use them properly and take care of them so they will last a long time.

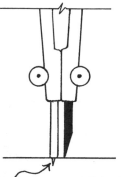

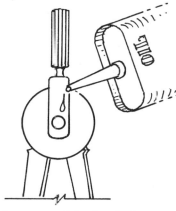

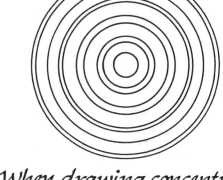

The points of ink or pencil compasses should be slightly longer than the marking point.

Never oil the joints of moving parts on any instrument. They will become too loose and you will be unable to hold your radius.

When drawing concentric circles, draw the smaller first and so on to the largest. The hole for the center gets larger with use, and it would be difficult to draw the small circles last.

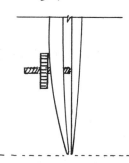

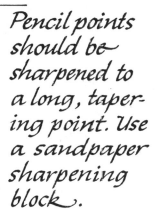

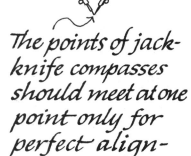

The two blades of the inking point of a compass should meet perfectly—never force the blades beyond the meeting point.

Pencil points should be sharpened to a long, tapering point. Use a sandpaper sharpening block.

The points of jack-knife compasses should meet at one point only for perfect alignment.

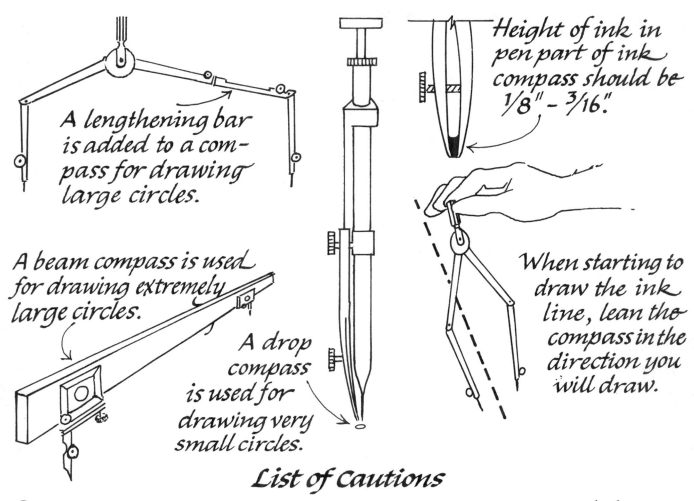

A lengthening bar is added to a compass for drawing large circles.

A beam compass is used for drawing extremely large circles.

A drop compass is used for drawing very small circles.

Height of ink in pen part of ink compass should be 1/8" - 3/16".

When starting to draw the ink line, lean the compass in the direction you will draw.

List of Cautions

①Never put either end of a wood-clinched pencil in your mouth (It is extremely unsanitary.)

②Never jab dividers into the drawing board.

③Never use the same thumb-tack holes to remount a drawing. Small pieces of paper tape are better for holding drawings down on the board.

④Never scrub a drawing all over with an eraser after finishing. It takes the life out of inked lines.

⑤Never begin work before wiping off table and instruments with a small brush.

⑥Never put bow instruments away before cleaning and relaxing the spring.

How to mark expensive drawing tools

When you buy your own expensive tools (drawing instruments, special pens, mechanical pencils, etc.), you should mark them with your name, initials, or some identifying mark (#). If you work in a large studio, your coworkers will borrow and they may forget to return them, just as you might do. To prevent confusion and possible violent arguments, mark your tools as shown below.

Paint your name or mark in contrasty color (to background) and then.............. spray your mark with a few layers of varnish spray. Make a mask to protect the other parts

PARK

VARNISH FIX

A push pin might work on some metals. Carefully scratch your mark on the side.

You might dip your item in paint, or paint an identifying mark – circle or band of color – around it.

GOLD PAINT

How to use poster and tempera color in a ruling pen

Poster and tempera watercolor can be thinned with water and put into a ruling pen with the aid of a brush.

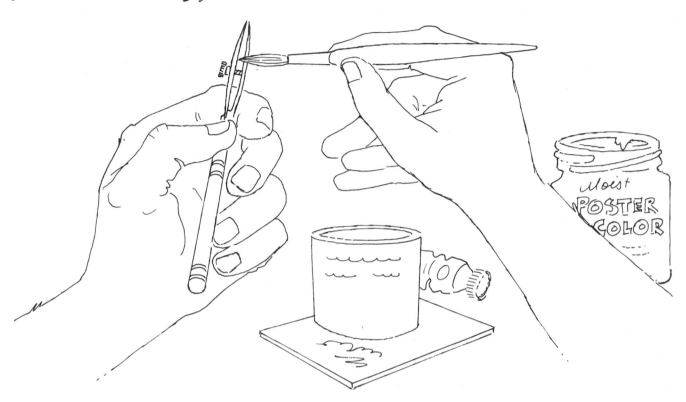

The ruling pen can then be used against a T square, triangle, and any other formed template you may design. From time to time, squeeze the blades of the ruling pen together and run the brush through the the blades to keep the color moist and wet enough to flow onto your drawing. While lines drawn in this manner may be a lighter value than the color you fill in later between the lines, the value change will be insignificant.

Other materials, such as oil paint, silk screen color, and acrylics can be inserted in a ruling pen and used in the same manner but you must work fast AND clean the pen thoroughly after you have used it.

How to help maintain technical pens

The best way to keep a technical pen in good working order is to follow the instructions that come with the pen when you buy it. If, for some reason, you have neglected to do so and you find that your pen needs cleaning, these instructions will help.

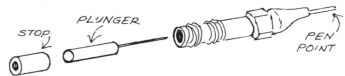

TWIST LEFT AND RIGHT GENTLY

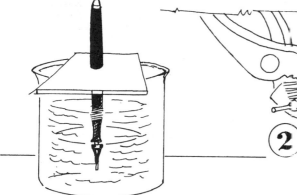

① Suspend the pen in warm detergent water or recommended ink solvent. Leave it suspended overnight.

② Next day, remove the pen tip assembly with a _very gentle_ back-and-forth action of the pliers, firmly gripping the pen assembly.

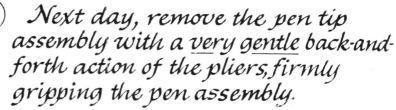

STOP PLUNGER PEN POINT

③ Separate the elements of the point and carefully clean them.

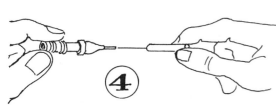

④ _Carefully_ use the plunger in reverse, as you would thread a needle, to clean the pen point. _Do not bend the plunger wire._

⑤ Fill the tip with warm water and carefully force a Q-tip into the open end of the point. Water should jet out when the point is clean. Dry all the parts and reassemble the pen.

How to make your own circle cutter

If you have a pencil compass, you can very easily make your own circle cutter. Your art store may have a blade to fit your compass where the lead goes, but if you had one and lost it or if you never had one — make one by following the instructions below.

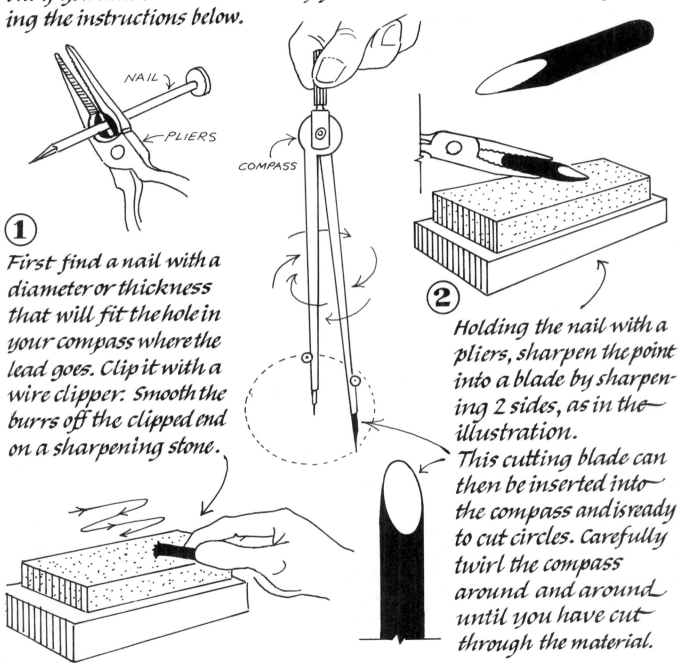

①
First find a nail with a diameter or thickness that will fit the hole in your compass where the lead goes. Clip it with a wire clipper. Smooth the burrs off the clipped end on a sharpening stone.

②
Holding the nail with a pliers, sharpen the point into a blade by sharpening 2 sides, as in the illustration.

This cutting blade can then be inserted into the compass and is ready to cut circles. Carefully twirl the compass around and around until you have cut through the material.

How to sharpen celluloid triangles

If edges of celluloid triangles get nicked and uneven, sharpen the edges as shown below and save triangles for much longer use.

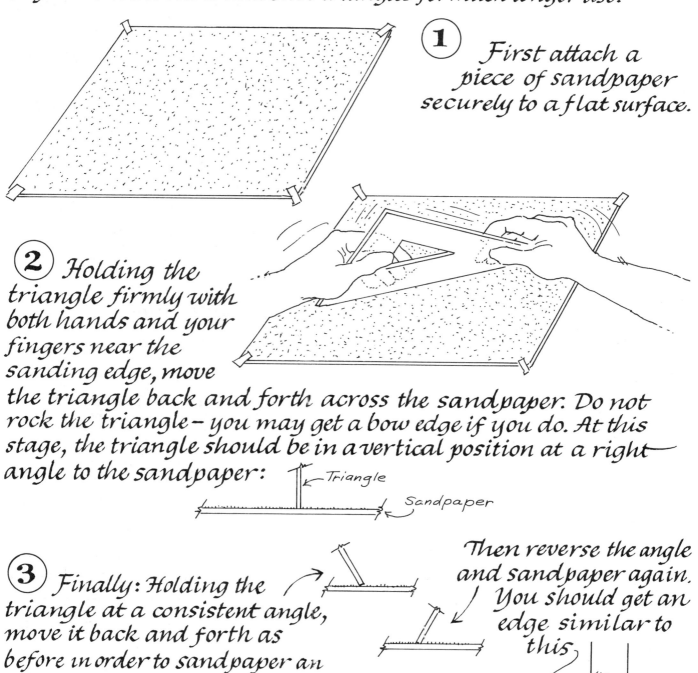

1 First attach a piece of sandpaper securely to a flat surface.

2 Holding the triangle firmly with both hands and your fingers near the sanding edge, move the triangle back and forth across the sandpaper. Do not rock the triangle – you may get a bow edge if you do. At this stage, the triangle should be in a vertical position at a right angle to the sandpaper:

Triangle

Sandpaper

3 Finally: Holding the triangle at a consistent angle, move it back and forth as before in order to sandpaper an edge on the side of the triangle.

Then reverse the angle and sandpaper again. You should get an edge similar to this.

Making Your Own Tools

How to maintain a constant uncommon angle on art work

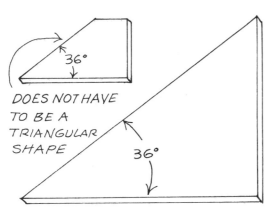

36°

DOES NOT HAVE
TO BE A
TRIANGULAR
SHAPE

36°

If you have the problem of maintaining a constant uncommon angle in making a drawing, carefully measure and cut a triangle of the desired angle from a piece of illustration board. The edge can be smoothed with a piece of sandpaper.

This triangle can be moved across your T square in the same manner as a regular plastic or metal triangle and need not always be in a triangular shape.

How to make an aid for cropping photographs

First, cut 2 large L-shapes out of heavy paper or light cardboard. Use them on a photograph, or on a drawing, to find the best area of the photo to reproduce or use, as shown on the top of the next page.

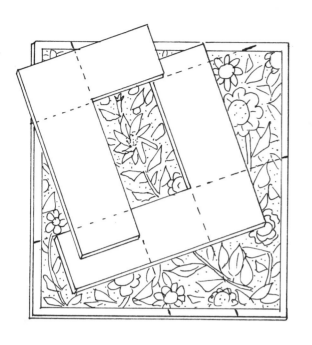

Move the 2 L-shaped cards around until you find the area of the photograph, or the drawing, you want to use. Once you establish the limits of the area, extend the sides to the edges of the photograph and mark for future use as shown with the dotted lines.

This method of using part of a picture is called "cropping."

How to make a device for drawing radiating lines

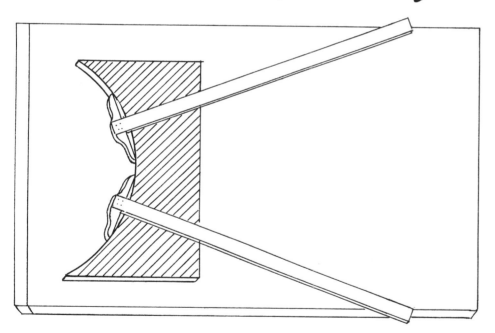

On a piece of heavy illustration board draw an arc of a large circle. Cut the piece of board out as shown at the left (shaded part), and secure it to the left side of the drawing board.

With the Tsquare against the curve, touching it at the extremes of the head of the Tsquare, draw radiating lines as desired. The arc can also be secured at the right side, the top, or at the bottom of the drawing board.

How to make a bridge from an old Tsquare

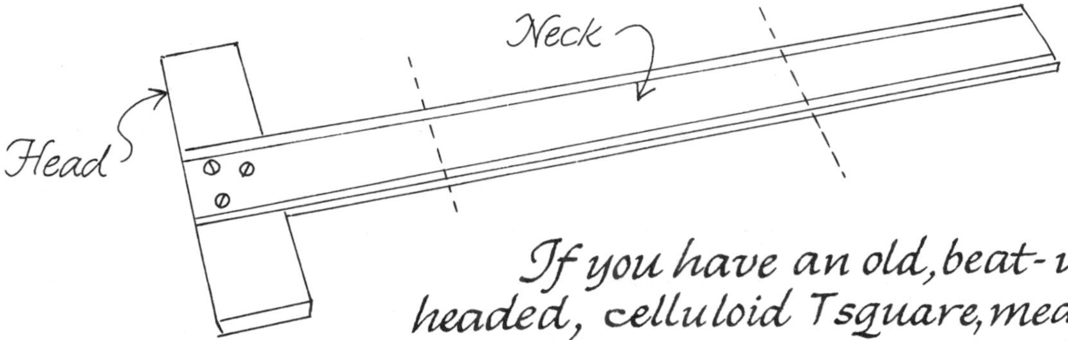

Neck

Head

If you have an old, beat-up, wooden-headed, celluloid Tsquare, measure off about a 12" section of the neck and cut it with a saw. (Pick a clean straight-edged section.)

Felt

Glue small strips of wood (about ½" square) to either side. When they are dry, glue small pieces of felt to the strip bottoms to prevent scuffs and scratches.

Your hand rests on the bridge, which is over the art work, and does not touch the art. The straight edge of the bridge can be used for drawing straight lines. Do not make the bridge too long or it might belly down and touch the art work. A bridge can also be made from any smooth strip of wood.

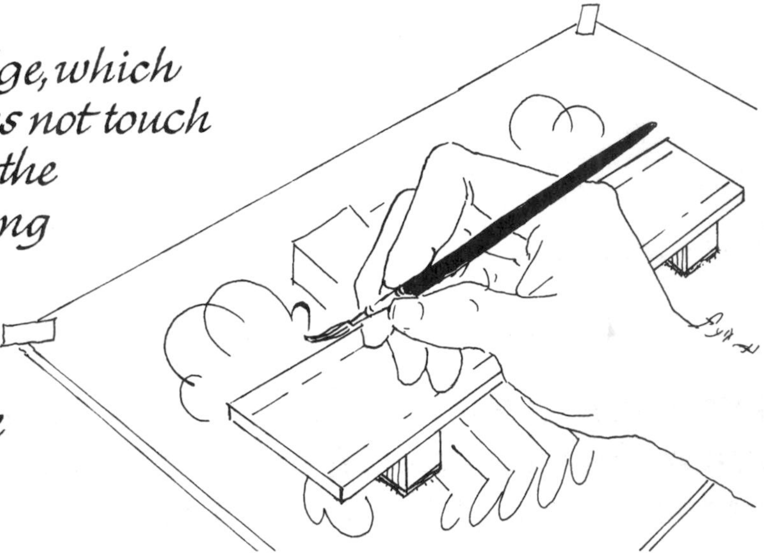

62

How to make an expedient proportional scale

In an extreme emergency when you have to enlarge something proportionately, the device below may help. It must be noted that, while it is a convenience, it is not precisely accurate.

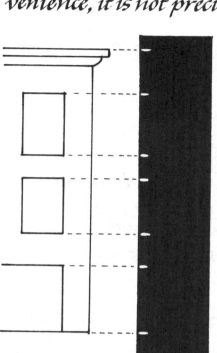

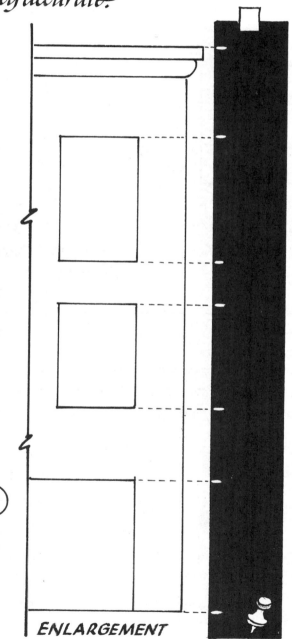

① On a wide elastic band mark off the elements you want to enlarge.

② Stretch the band to the overall length desired, mark off the points, and redraw the enlargement.

ENLARGEMENT

It cannot be emphasized too much that this is not a precise and accurate enlargement BUT it may help if close is good enough.

Secure ends with tape or push pins.

How to make your own "ruler"

There may be an occasion when you want to measure something, or establish a proportion and do not have a convenient measuring device handy. It is a simple matter to make your own ruler and obtain the proportions you want.

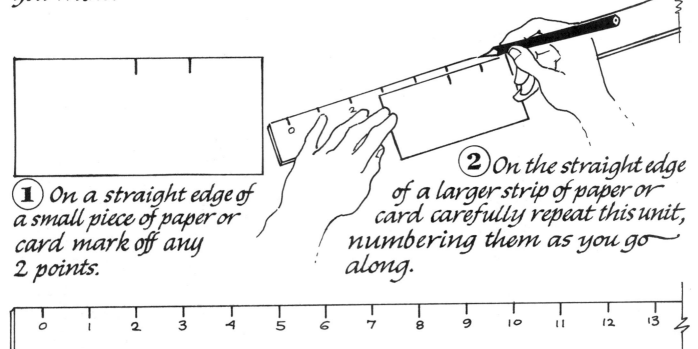

① On a straight edge of a small piece of paper or card mark off any 2 points.

② On the straight edge of a larger strip of paper or card carefully repeat this unit, numbering them as you go along.

③ You have now made your own measuring device which can be used to measure units of relative distances.

PHOTO

MECHANICAL

DO YOU HAVE XOU

In the example to the left you want to reduce the photo to a photostat the width of B on the marks on the mechanical. Suppose that the photo measures 10 units and your mechanical area measures 5 units, using your "ruler." You would now order a photostat for 50% reduction (10:5).

Household Helpers
How to use art supplies found in the medicine cabinet

Many of the items found in the bathroom medicine cabinet can be used as tools to aid the graphic artist. Examples and their uses are shown below.

① 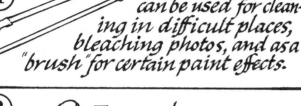 Q-tips and swabs can be used for cleaning in difficult places, bleaching photos, and as a "brush" for certain paint effects.

② 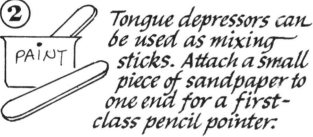 Tongue depressors can be used as mixing sticks. Attach a small piece of sandpaper to one end for a first-class pencil pointer.

Talcum powder dusts and dries hands on wet or humid days. ③

④ Ammonia can be used to thin down or clean waterproof ink.

An eyedropper can ⑤ be used to measure liquids and fill pens.

TONGUE DEPRESSOR
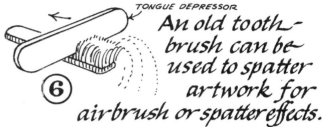 An old tooth-brush can be used to spatter artwork for air-brush or spatter effects. ⑥

⑦ Cotton balls with rubber-cement thinner are great for cleaning purposes and for rubbing charcoal and pastel drawings for effect.

Hydrogen peroxide is great for bleaching out areas of a photo. Use Q-tips or swabs to apply it. ⑧

⑨ Adhesive tapes can be used to mark bottles and patch busted paint tubes, as can nail polish.

How to make a convenient pegboard holder for tools

A small pegboard and frame
can be constructed to be positioned
to the left of your drawing board, and hooks installed
where you want them. It is a handy arrangement
to hold tools frequently used in your daily work.

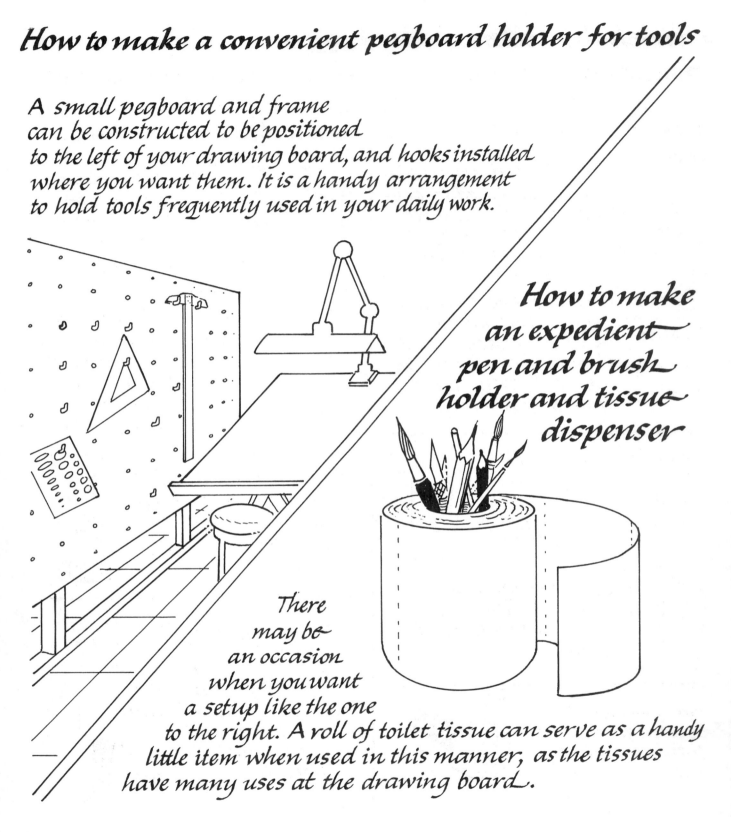

How to make an expedient pen and brush holder and tissue dispenser

There
may be
an occasion
when you want
a setup like the one
to the right. A roll of toilet tissue can serve as a handy
little item when used in this manner, as the tissues
have many uses at the drawing board.

Inks
Tips on using inks

STICK INK

NET STRING

You can make your own ink.*Sticks of ink and a heavy slate dish can be used with water. After gently grinding, the longer the darker, the ink is filtered with a wet string. This thin ink is great for writing calligraphy or drawing fine line art.

* STICKS ARE AVAILABLE IN ART STORES.

ALCOHOL

RAG

VELLUM

Vellum can be washed with a little alcohol and ink adheres to it much easier.

DR. BRISCOE'S VERMILLION

MAGENTA

RED

Red ink or dye is sometimes much thinner than black, allowing you to use it on a fine line drawing. It reproduces just like black.

Writing Ink

DRAWING INK

As a rule you should not mix together 2 different kinds of ink, such as writing ink and waterproof drawing ink. In writing calligraphy that will be erased later a few drops of waterproof ink mixed with writing ink is sometimes good. Throw away excess when finished.

67

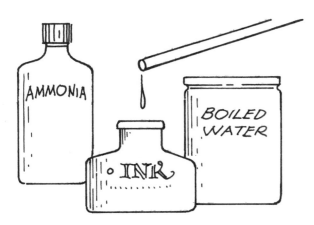

Thin ink with distilled or boiled water, ammonia, or alcohol. Since waterproof ink has shellac in it, alcohol will thin it. Do not use faucet water — it will smell in a short time after capping.

Wash hands frequently when working with ink, especially in writing calligraphy. Greasy hands leave grease spots on paper and pen will skip and blur.

Be _absolutely sure_ that ink is _dry_ before erasing. Seems trite, but the above happens too frequently in art studios.

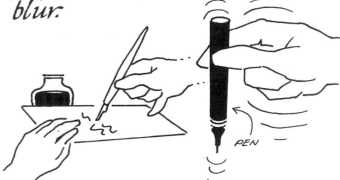

ALWAYS test ink (pen) on scratch paper before using. Jiggle and wipe technical pens until they work.

Always put top back on ink immediately after using — it will prevent drying out and if knocked over will not make a mess.

How to "mark time" on ink bottles

All artists who work with ink know how frustrating it is to pick up and use a bottle of old ink just as they are about to ink in a drawing.

To avoid this, mark your bottles with the date on which you receive them. You can write the date on a small piece of white tape and adhere it to the side of the bottle or container.

How to make a home-made humidor for technical pens

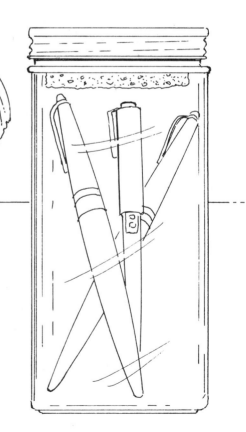

Take an old clean jar with a screw-on top. On the inside of the jar top, glue a small sponge, using waterproof glue. (Be sure that the jar size will accommodate technical pens.)

Keep the sponge wet (not dripping) and close the jar with the technical pens that you use, with ink in them, inside. They will stay workable as long as the sponge is damp and the top is tightly screwed on. This is a great way to store pens for weekends. Be sure that the tip ends of the pens are up.

69

Paint
How to keep watercolors moist

Expensive watercolors, designers' colors, tempera, or other water-based paint can be kept moist and workable indefinitely if you use the following suggestion. This will also save you money because you will not waste paint.

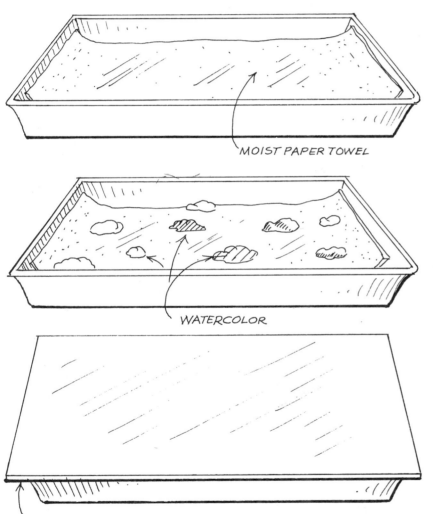

MOIST PAPER TOWEL

WATERCOLOR

STIFF CARDBOARD OR MOIST PAPER TOWEL

Line the bottom of a shallow cookie pan, or similar waterproof container, with a paper towel — the kind that is found in wall dispensers.

Moisten the towel but do not saturate it with water. The towel can be kept damp with periodic applications of small amounts of water. Squeeze paint onto the damp towel as you need it. Arrange the colors as you would on any palette, allowing enough space between the colors for intermixing other colors.

Place a damp towel or a heavy flat oversize card over the top of the cookie tin for the weekend. Your paint should be moist and ready for use when you get back.

How to prevent watercolor caps from sticking

One of the most annoying things that can happen to a designer or water-color artist is to pick up a tube of paint that he or she has used before and not to be able to get the cap off. He tries a match, hot water, and twisting back and forth with pliers, but it will not come off. Here are 2 suggestions that may help you in this situation.

Replace the plastic caps with metal ones. When discarding old tubes, save all the metal caps—they will be less likely to stick to the top of the tube.

A little lubricating jelly painted on the threads of the tube and cap will help keep caps from freezing shut again.

You can buy in a drug store for a modest price a small tube of lubricating jelly. It is water-soluble and extremely slow in drying.

Glycerine (drug store) can also be used. It, too, is water-soluble and slow-drying. It is sometimes used to help keep colors from drying too fast.

How to prevent mold from forming in jars of watercolor

Mold forms in jars of paint that haven't been opened for awhile because of bacterial activity. There are a few hints below on what you can do to minimize this action.

Instead of using regular faucet water (with bacteria) for thinning color, boil some water (killing bacteria) and keep this boiled water in a small container in the studio for thinning colors in jars.

STOVE

OFF OFF OFF

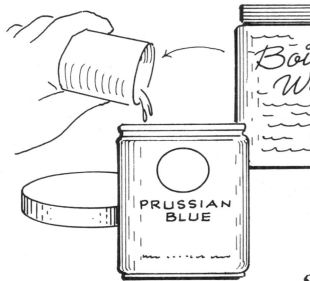

Boiled Water

Or use distilled water.

PRUSSIAN BLUE

DENATURED ALCOHOL

KEEP AWAY FROM CHILDREN

Blues and browns are especially prone to bacterial action.

Of course, jars should be tightly sealed when not in use. Bacteria in the air may get in if they are not tight.

Van Dyke Brown

A few drops of denatured alcohol will help prevent bacterial build-up in jars.

72

Some tips on storing oil paint and cleaning brushes

Preserving leftover oil paints is the concern of everyone who works in oil. Here are some suggestions for "saving" them for short times—saving the artist some money as well.

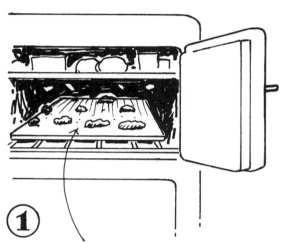

① Store them in the freezer—they will keep indefinitely.

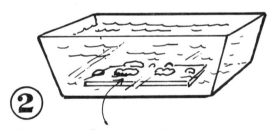

② Use a glass palette and submerge the entire palette in a convenient large pan of water. Good for a week but not much longer—some oxidation with the pigment does take place in the water.

③ Use old plastic pill containers. Seal the lid edges with tape. Old aluminum airtight cans, which hold 35 mm film, can also be used.

④ Oil brushes should be cleaned after each painting session. Rub excess paint onto a rag, wash in turpentine and wash with white soap and warm water many times. Kerosene or mineral spirits may be used.

The addition of a small piece of screen on the bottom of the jar may help rub out some of the paint from the heel of the brush.

How to maintain poster color or tempera

Once a month, remove all jar tops and add water. This will keep the paint from drying, so that it will always be ready for work.

An eye dropper is a handy tool for adding water

If the paint smells sour, add a drop or two of denatured alcohol.

If the paint dusts off the job when it is dry, add a drop or two of mucilage or glue to the jar.

If the paint is chalky, add a drop of glycerin to each jar. It will also slow down the drying time of the paint.

Gum arabic and oxgall can also be added to the paint if the paint does not adhere to the surface.

How to open stubborn jars and tubes

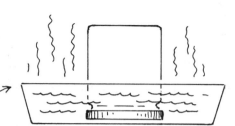

Soak the bottle upside down in hot water overnight.

Impossible tubes: Prick tube, use paint, and tape the hole when you're finished.

Use a small strip of sandpaper from your pencil pointer, wrap it around the jar's cap, and twist in both directions.

Hit the cap with light glancing taps in the direction of the unscrew.

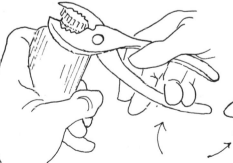

Regular pliers and nut or lobster crackers can be used.

Splash hot water on the bottle's neck.

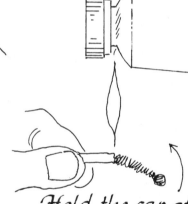

Hold the cap at the tip of a flame from a match or lighter.

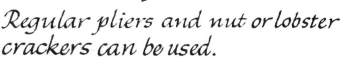

How to make a paint "hell-box"

The word hell-box came from the printing trades. Used metal in the printer's shop was thrown into a hell box and melted down for reuse in casting new type. You can use old watercolor paint residue in your water jar and chips from your color spread cards to make your own hell box.

Residue from water jars and scrapings from palettes are saved in the hellbox. Gum water (you can buy it in art stores) or gum arabic crystals (art store) can be added to give it body and an adhesive quality. The resulting color will surprise you when used from the hellbox. We dare you to try and match it by mixing your own.

WATER JAR

SPATULA

RESIDUE FROM WATER JAR

LID TO HELL BOX

HELL BOX

GUM WATER

A

GUM ARABIC CRYSTALS

SPATULA

SCRAPINGS OF PAINT FROM PALETTE OR SPREAD CARD

HELL BOX

LID

How to make a "stationary" card palette for mixing paint

When you are preparing your brush by pointing it on a spread card or palette, it is very annoying to have the card move around. On large jobs a large "immovable" palette would be used and you would not have this problem. Here's a suggestion for those small jobs where a small card is used for preparing your paint and brush.

Small bar of metal ¼"–½" thick, with round or smooth edges

MAGNETIC CLIP

SPREAD CARD

A magnetic clip is attached to the upper part of a small, heavy metal bar. The clip holds your spread card, which can easily be replaced when necessary. Your card will not move around the drawing board with this setup. Here are two other simple methods of "holding" your spread card.

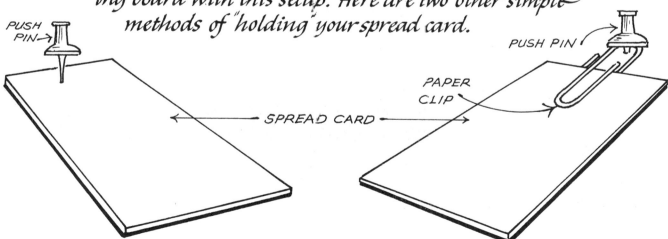

PUSH PIN

PUSH PIN

PAPER CLIP

SPREAD CARD

Tape
Tape tips

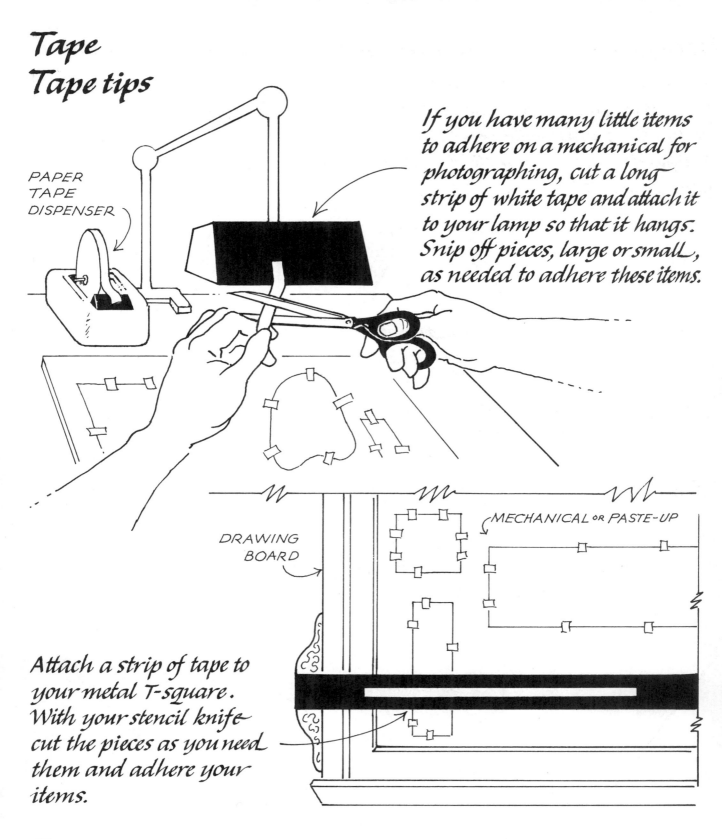

PAPER TAPE DISPENSER

If you have many little items to adhere on a mechanical for photographing, cut a long strip of white tape and attach it to your lamp so that it hangs. Snip off pieces, large or small, as needed to adhere these items.

DRAWING BOARD

MECHANICAL OR PASTE-UP

Attach a strip of tape to your metal T-square. With your stencil knife cut the pieces as you need them and adhere your items.

How to make dried-up masking tape like new again

If you have an old roll of paper or masking tape that has dried and stuck together, follow the instructions below to make it almost like new again.

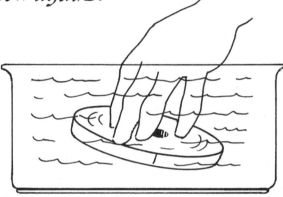

① Soak the roll in water for about 10 seconds.

② Then heat it in the oven until it is warmed through. Set the oven at 250°. It should take a few minutes. Peel off some tape as a test. If it is beyond saving — heave it in file 13.

How to find ends of tapes on rolls easily

ROLL

END OF TAPE TURNED, FLATTENED, AND PASTED TO ITSELF

It is very annoying to pick up a roll of tape and pick around with your fingernails to try to find the end. By simply turning the end back on itself about ¼" when you have finished using it you will have no trouble finding the end next time.

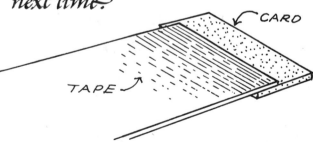

CARD

TAPE

Another simple method is to adhere a small piece of card to the end of the tape.

Rubber Cement
Using rubber cement and wax

Rubber cement is available in both 1-coat and 2-coat versions. One-coat cement is applied to only one surface, usually your artwork. For 2-coat cement both the artwork and the receiving surface are coated. One-coat is quicker to use, but artwork is more difficult to adjust while being positioned. Use a small square of rubber, called a rubber cement pick-up, to remove excess cement. Don't use your fingers since they can leave dirt on your mechanical and the cement may harm your skin. If your rubber cement is too thick, thin it with rubber cement thinner. Use a spout can to control the amount of thinner. With both rubber cement and rubber cement thinner work in a well-ventilated room and store both products away from heat.

Wax is an alternative to rubber cement. It is non-toxic and non-flammable. It can be applied with a hand-waxer or a larger machine that coats sheets 8½" x 11" or larger. Excess wax can be scraped off with a razor blade or dissolved with rubber cement thinner.

Rubber cement yellows and stains with age. Waxed items can move around or come loose when exposed to high or prolonged heat.

Gluesticks are a simple, inexpensive alternative to wax and rubber cement. But excess glue is more difficult to clean up and repositioning artwork is harder.

Mark "close" and "open" on rubber-cement dispenser

If you have a rubber-cement dispenser with a valve at the end of the spout, you can develop an easy way of opening and closing it as you use it. Simply pick it up at the valve end and twist it open to use. When finished, grasp it again at the valve and twist closed when returning it to your tabouret.

A simple twist of the thumb and forefinger will do the trick.

Attach a piece of paper tape to the side. Mark it "close" and "open" with arrows.

← CLOSE
OPEN →

How to get longer life from a rubber cement pickup

While a rubber-cement pickup is a relatively inexpensive item, you can prolong its life and save some $ in the long run by trimming the collected rubber cement from the pickup with a pair of scissors.

After cleaning in this manner the pickup is almost as good as new and can last for years...

...and you save money, too.

What to do if you spill rubber cement

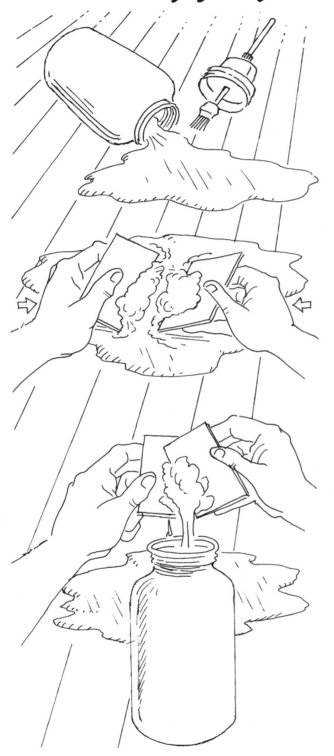

If rubber cement is spilled, act fast. First "right" the container and stand it away from the action.

With two small stiff cards, start gathering the cement as shown. If it was spilled on a clean surface, return the recovered cement to the container. Repeat until all cement is saved or cleaned from the floor.

If cement is spilled on a dirty area, place the picked-up cement into a coffee container (or on a piece of newspaper) and deposit it in a trash can.

Dry cement on the floor can also be picked up with a rubber cement pick-up.

Work fast !!!

Keep a supply of small stiff cards (3" x 5" approximately) always handy.

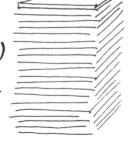

How to make a paper funnel

There may be times when you need a funnel in a hurry. You may be working on a job and need rubber-cement thinner in your dispenser can. You need a funnel and can't find one. If you follow the instructions below, a good temporary funnel can be made in a matter of minutes.

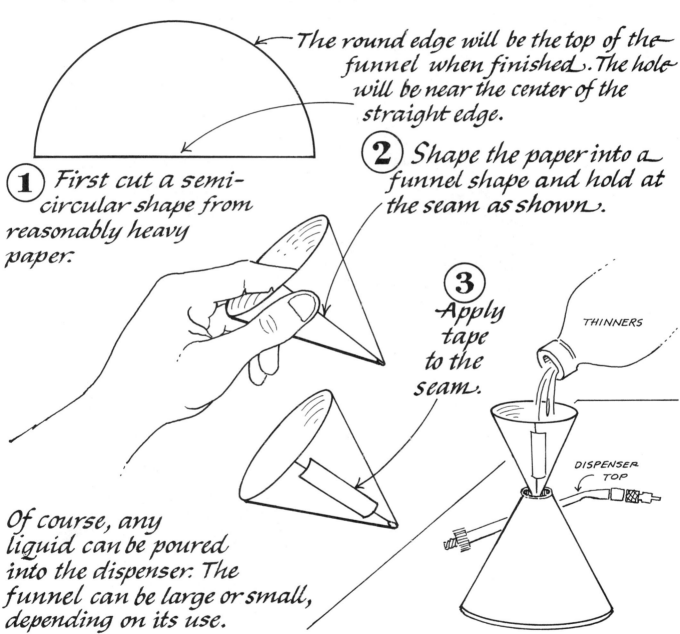

The round edge will be the top of the funnel when finished. The hole will be near the center of the straight edge.

(1) First cut a semi-circular shape from reasonably heavy paper.

(2) Shape the paper into a funnel shape and hold at the seam as shown.

(3) Apply tape to the seam.

THINNERS

DISPENSER TOP

Of course, any liquid can be poured into the dispenser. The funnel can be large or small, depending on its use.

Containers
How to hold and remove tops from bottles and jars

In attempting to remove tops from ink bottles and jars of paint, etc., do not suspend the bottles in the air. Hold them _firmly_ _on_ _a_ _solid_ _table top_ and then remove the top by twisting back and forth. _Never_ open jars or bottles over artwork or illustration board.

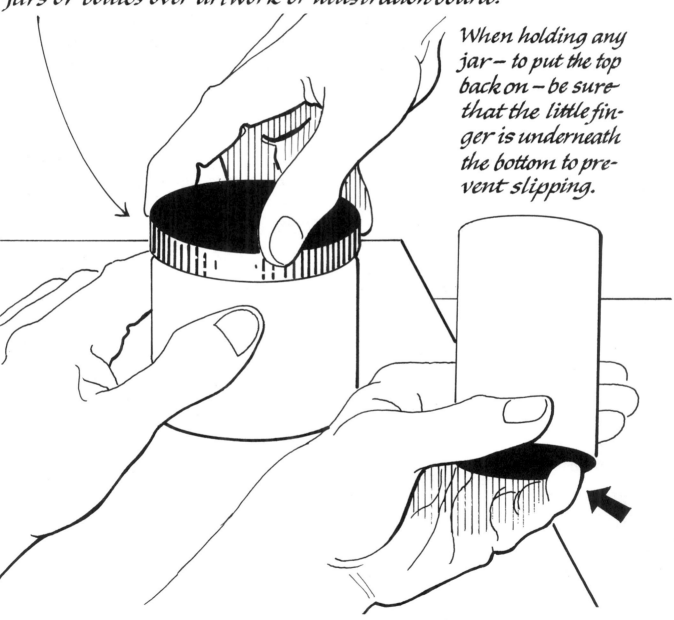

When holding any jar — to put the top back on — be sure that the little finger is underneath the bottom to prevent slipping.

How to make inexpensive water and paint containers

Common household plastic containers can be cut down to make no-cost water and paint containers. They can be as large as you want, depending on the size container you start with.

Cut a large plastic container to make a large water "jar." Measure and mark the cutting edge (indicated by the dotted line above) and cut with the mat knife.

Smaller containers can be cut from small plastic bottles. Pill containers are great for small amounts of mixed colors. A cover of wax paper with a rubber band will keep the color moist overnight.

How household plastic containers can be used as water holders for outdoor watercolors

If you take "field trips" to the country to paint in watercolor and are not near a ready water supply (stream, pond, etc.), you can carry the water with you in one of the household plastic squeeze containers. They come in large and small sizes, can be easily cleaned, and will not leak if the tops are secured.

One can be cut down for a water container while you work.

Paper
How to remove plies from the back of illustration board

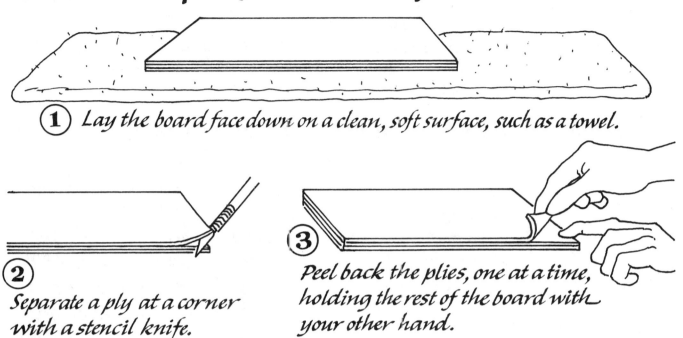

① Lay the board face down on a clean, soft surface, such as a towel.

② Separate a ply at a corner with a stencil knife.

③ Peel back the plies, one at a time, holding the rest of the board with your other hand.

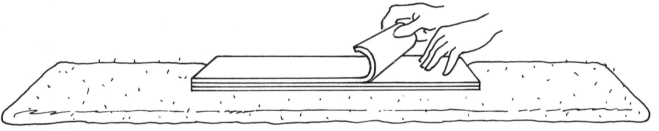

④ Remove the ply carefully. Remove all loose pieces with the knife held almost parallel to the board.

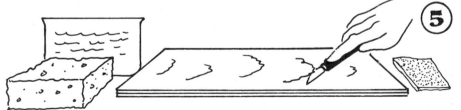

⑤ In removing ply it may help to dampen the back with a sponge and water.

When dry, the entire back surface can be gently smoothed by rubbing it with sandpaper.

How to compensate for thick boards

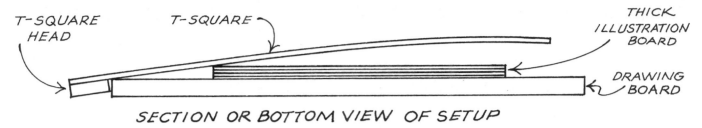

T-SQUARE HEAD

T-SQUARE

THICK ILLUSTRATION BOARD

DRAWING BOARD

SECTION OR BOTTOM VIEW OF SETUP

Sometimes it is awkward to manipulate your T-square when working on thick items on your drawing board. To compensate for this thickness, simply cut a strip of heavy board (illustration board) and attach it to the extreme left of your board. The T-square will then ride on this strip making your work much easier. Be sure that the head of the T-square can still "grab" the left side of the drawing board.

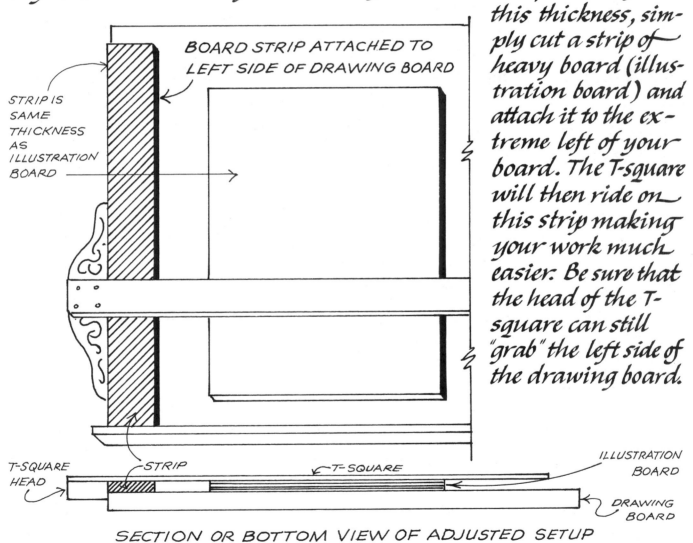

BOARD STRIP ATTACHED TO LEFT SIDE OF DRAWING BOARD

STRIP IS SAME THICKNESS AS ILLUSTRATION BOARD

T-SQUARE HEAD

STRIP

T-SQUARE

ILLUSTRATION BOARD

DRAWING BOARD

SECTION OR BOTTOM VIEW OF ADJUSTED SETUP

88

How to prevent paper cuts while handling sheets of paper or thin cards

Thin white cotton gloves can be worn to minimize paper cuts when handling large amounts of paper or thin cards. If you are working on a large, thin illustration board and must move it around a lot, you can also wear the gloves. If you do not want to remove them, cut off the fingers of the glove so that you have complete freedom in using art tools.

They can be worn while filing large amounts of cards or papers. If you have ever had a nasty paper cut, you will wear gloves the next time.

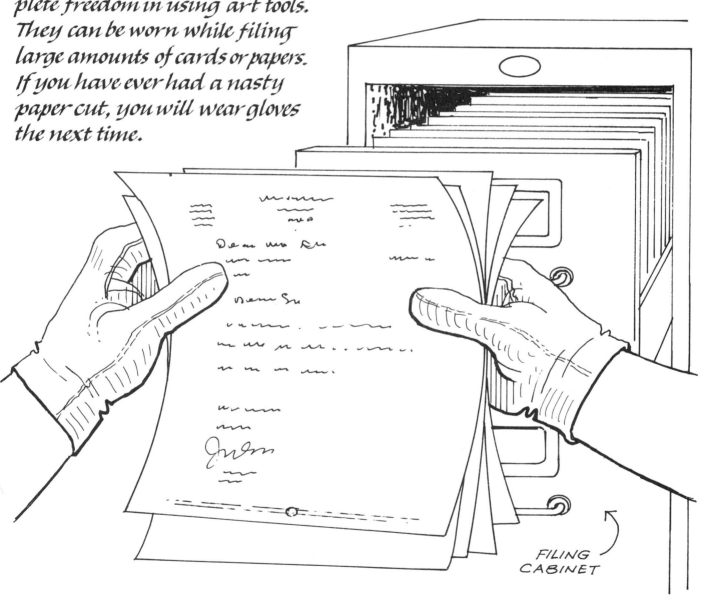

FILING
CABINET

How to save watercolor paper

If you are using good, expensive watercolor paper and paint a bad painting or have an accident that ruins the painting, don't throw the paper away. It can be "saved" for another painting. Soak the entire painting in a bathtub or sink full of warm, clean water. You can agitate the painting by gently rubbing with a soft rag or brush. Try not to disturb the fibers of the paper.

When finished washing, hang the paper to dry and then stretch it for a new painting. Blotting it with large blotters may aid in drying.

The surface can again be agitated from time to time with a soft rag and bristle brush. Papers cleaned in this manner can be used more than twice.

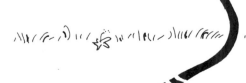

A regular garden hose can be used to gently spray the color from the paper.

Lettering
How to identify regular, condensed and extended letter proportions

The lettering on the inscription of the Trajan Column in Rome (113 AD) has estabished the criteria for the most beautiful letter proportions (width to height of individual letters and letters to each other) for centuries. Here are some of those letter proportions.

ROMANVS

Everyone concerned with the design or use of letters or type should study these letters (on the inscription) as the ideal for the classic form. All alphabets designed since then are regular. Deviations – making them wider (extended) or narrower (condensed) – of the designed alphabet should be understood.

A NORMAL — This is one letter of a designed alphabet. It would be the normal set (width to height relationship)

A CONDENSED — The same letter (style and height remaining the same). This would be the condensed form of that alphabet. All the other letters of the normal alphabet would also be narrower than normal.

A EXTENDED — The same letter (style and height remaining the same). This would be the expanded or extended form of the alphabet.

Design your own style of alphabet and then design a condensed and an extended version. The only letter that remains the same in all three versions is the letter "I."

How to distinguish between blackletter, text, Old English, sans serif, and Gothic letter styles

The above terms have confused designers and students of lettering for a long time. The descriptions below will help you understand the differences.

The more easily understood names for these styles are

Blackletter

For many centuries (10th – 13th) this was the true gothic letter. The Goths had left the scene long before, but the lettering was used on Gothic architecture and was called "Gothic." In northern Europe it was compressed and angular. In southern Europe it was softer, slightly expanded, and more curvilinear. It was very black on the page – so "blackletter" describes it more accurately than Gothic. Another name is Text (short for Textura), derived from the woven appearance of a page of blackletter (like a textile). Old English is simply another name for Blackletter. The capitals are very decorative; and the style is used frequently today on formal announcements, certificates and religious printing.

sans serif

means without serifs. Serifs are the tiny strokes that extend from the stems and other main strokes of a letter. American typographers called it Gothic. Some American typeface names are Franklin Gothic, News Gothic, Alternate Gothic and Globe Gothic. In Europe it is often called "Grotesk".

Futura type (designed by Paul Renner in Germany around 1928) is based on classic proportions. It is still a much used style. It is simple and unadorned. Many distorted forms of it appear in type specimen books. "Gothic" is a misnomer for this style.

Difference between written and built-up lettering

All lettering can be classified under 2 types by method of accomplishing the lettering – written and built-up. The differences are shown below.

Informal Script { This lettering is freely written with a pen or brush and is done directly – what you write is the lettering. It can be retouched.

Brush { This style is done with a brush, pointed or flat-edged. It can be re-touched.

Calligraphy { Calligraphic writing is done with a flat-edged tool and the result is immediately finished letter-ing. It should not be retouched.

All the above lettering is <u>written</u>. There are, of course, many variations of the styles.

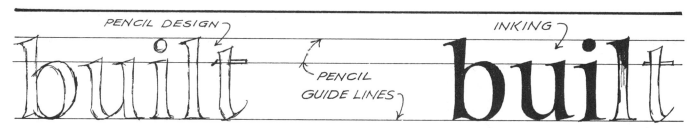

PENCIL DESIGN
INKING
PENCIL GUIDE LINES

<u>Built-up</u> letters are first carefully designed in pencil and correct-ed until they are just what you want. Then the letters are care-fully outlined in ink, using a pen or brush, and filled in (made solid black) with a brush (usually). They are retouched – first with ink and then with white opaque watercolor – with a brush.

How to identify the major styles of lettering

Old Style Roman

Curved letters have stress on the bias

The height of the letter is 9 to 11 times the thickness of the stem (the heavy stroke). Hairline stroke (the thin stroke) is about ½ the size of thick stroke. Serifs are heavy, rounded and cupped. The style has a hand-drawn look.

Modern Roman

Curved letters have vertical stress

The set of this letter is the same as with the old style. There is great contrast between the stem and the hairline strokes. Serifs are hairline, with no fillets. It looks mechanically drawn.

Sans (without) Serif

The set is the same as o.s.* It looks like the same thickness of stroking throughout. There are no serifs. When the set changes from classic roman, the style is called grotesk, gothic or a number of other styles, all of which have no serifs. *old style roman

Formal Script

About

This form is slanted, joined, and looks written, although it is carefully designed. It is sometimes called Spencerian after Charles Spencer, an early writing master.

Informal Script

Friends

This is a casual, vertical written form – with no definite requirements other than that it can be read.

Calligraphy

Manch

The slanted, written formal letter is done with a flat-edged tool (chisel-edged pencil, brush, or pen.)

Black Text

Medí

This true Gothic lettering is medieval. It is heavy, vertical, quadrangular and condensed.

Square Serif

This letter has square or slab serifs and a roman set. It is mechanical-looking.

Italic

bint

Non-joining, slanted formal letters are carefully designed and named after "Italy," where they originated.

Decorative

Here obviously ornamented, the letters can be a basic form with ornaments and shading.

These remarks are very general. More study of the subject would be required to become an accomplished letterer.

How to identify parts of letters correctly

Anyone concerned with designing, not just letterers, should be able to identify and name the parts of letters correctly. Here is the correct terminology for roman letter forms.

Terms refer to those parts of letters encircled when circles or ovals are shown.

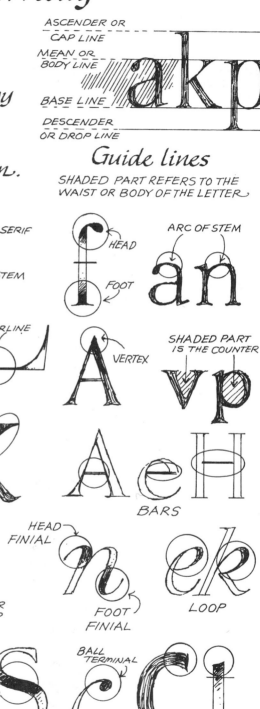

ASCENDER OR CAP LINE
MEAN OR BODY LINE
BASE LINE
DESCENDER OR DROP LINE

Guide lines

SHADED PART REFERS TO THE WAIST OR BODY OF THE LETTER

CIRCULAR BOWL

OVAL BOWL

BIASED STRESS

VERTICAL STRESS

SERIF

STEM

HAIRLINE

HEAD

FOOT

ARC OF STEM

SHADED PART IS THE COUNTER

BRACKETED SERIF

SLAB OR SQUARE SERIF

HAIRLINE SERIF

CUPPED SERIF

VERTEX

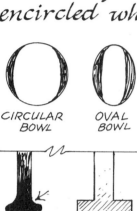

TAIL

ARMS

BARS

NICK

CROSS BAR

EAR

LINK or NECK

LOWER LOOP

HEAD FINIAL

FOOT FINIAL

LOOP

SWASH LETTERS
IDENTIFIED BY HAVING FLOUR-ISHED TAILS AND TERMINALS

BEAK

EYE

SPINE

BALL TERMINAL

TERMINALS

How to distinguish typefaces by lower case "g"

To distinguish among typefaces focus on these key letters: G, K, M, Q, R and W; and a, e, g, k, t and y. Determine if the typeface is roman, italic or other; and, if roman, if it is serif or sans serif; and finally, if serif, what kind.

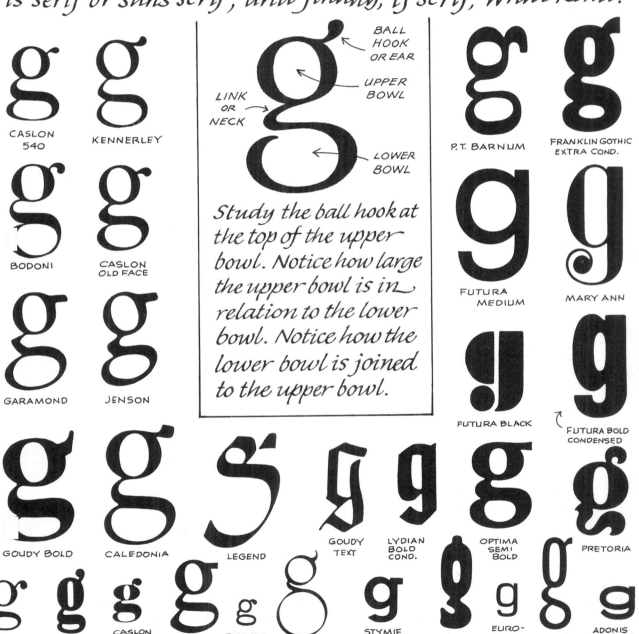

BALL HOOK OR EAR

UPPER BOWL

LINK OR NECK

LOWER BOWL

Study the ball hook at the top of the upper bowl. Notice how large the upper bowl is in relation to the lower bowl. Notice how the lower bowl is joined to the upper bowl.

CASLON 540

KENNERLEY

P.T. BARNUM

FRANKLIN GOTHIC EXTRA COND.

BODONI

CASLON OLD FACE

FUTURA MEDIUM

MARY ANN

GARAMOND

JENSON

FUTURA BLACK

FUTURA BOLD CONDENSED

GOUDY BOLD

CALEDONIA

LEGEND

GOUDY TEXT

LYDIAN BOLD COND.

OPTIMA SEMI BOLD

PRETORIA

CENTURY EXPANDED

CONTACT BOLD

CASLON BLACK

TIMES ROMAN

BULLETIN TYPE-WRITER

CELTIC

STYMIE BOLD

HEROLD REKLAME

EURO-STILE

NEWS GOTHIC EXTRA COND.

ADONIS EXTENDED

How to sketch classic roman capital letters

The _set_ of a letter is the relationship of its width to its height. The beauty of lettering depends, therefore, on the artist's understanding of the sets of all letters according to classic roman tradition, accepted through the ages as the ideal of beautiful letter form. The basic sets of those classic forms are shown here. Anyone applying this information will be well on his or her way to accomplishing good lettering. Other factors of lettering are important, but the set is the most important one.

Square set
Limits fall within a square.

Narrow set
Width is less than a square.

Wide set
Width is more than a square.

"M" is another wide-set letter

The 2 thin letters

Rest of square-set letters

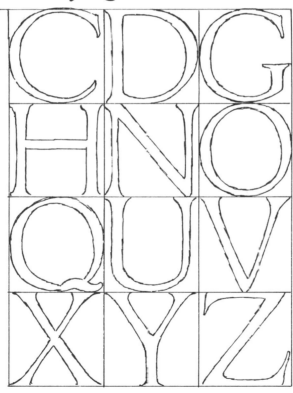

Rest of narrow-set letters

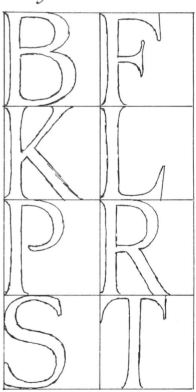

These sets are to be followed whether the letter is sans serif, speedball, square serif, or any other type of letter.

Optical illusions in lettering

When you letter words, phrases, or simply letters in design, you must be aware of the illusions that occur with letters and how you can compensate for them to make the lettering look right. This is true for rough, comprehensive, or finished lettering. These are the essential illusions.

Parts of letters that have points must come beyond the guide-lines, or they will look too short.

All curves of letters must go beyond the guide-lines, or they will look smaller.

On block letters certain parts, such as those above, must be drawn wider than the down-stroke thickness.

On some letters the outside down strokes should converge toward points so that white space can be drawn and letters will not get spotty as in circled parts of letter to the right.

In block letters the horizontals are slightly thinner than the verticals so that they look like they are the same weight as shown above.

The vertical strokes of capitals are heavier than the verticals of lowercase. If they are drawn with the same weight, the cap width will appear to be thinner.

In slanted italics and scripts, the oval parts of letters tilt at a different direction than the down stroke. Otherwise they will look awkward as in the example above.

98

How to letter-space, word-space, and line-space

Spacing type or lettering is a matter of eye judgment. The "rules" below will help you develop this sense. Lettering is demonstrated, but the same "rules" of legibility apply to type.

Letter space is the area between <u>letters</u> of a word from top guideline (cap line) to bottom line (base or aligning line). These areas are easy to evaluate when the edges of the letters are vertical, biased, or elliptical from top to bottom. For the open-sided letters such as C, E, Z, etc. judge ½ of the inside space to the adjacent letter to figure your area.

Assuming that the letters above form a word, all the cross-hatched areas should look the same (equal in area) to the eye — 2 straights, as in "IN" above, are farthest apart, and 2 curves (OC) are closest. Letter space is the same throughout the entire copy — no matter how many lines.

Word space is the space between <u>words</u> in continuous copy — can be different but not vastly different — in order to align the right hand margin.

THE QUICK BROWN FOX
JUMPS OVER LAZY DOGS

In the drawing above word space is the shaded area between words. Normal word space is the width of the letter "c".

Line space is the white space <u>between</u> <u>lines</u> of lettering or type (shaded part below). The distances from base line to base line are equal. Never have more word space than line space.

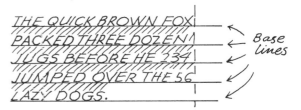

THE QUICK BROWN FOX
PACKED THREE DOZEN
JUGS BEFORE HE 234
JUMPED OVER THE 56
LAZY DOGS.

Base lines

How to paste down type on a curved alignment

In pencil, draw the curve on which you desire to position the type on your mechanical.

Trace this curve on a piece of tracing paper, lay it over the type proof and trace the letters, turning the paper frequently to have the letters align on the curve as you want. You should have a tracing that looks like this, when finished.

Trim the type line close at the top and bottom and, by inspection, slit with a sharp knife from the edges in (shown below with dotted lines) according to how the letters turn. Attach the tracing to the mechan-

THE QUICK BROWN FOX JUMPS OVER THE MOON

ical, matching the curves, and use it as a guide. Apply rubber cement to the back of the sliced type proof and also to the curved line on the mechanical. Use a tissue slip sheet under the proof as you dry mount it down along the curve. A pair of tweezers will help. When you are finished cementing the proof down, clean up and...

THE QUICK BROWN FOX JUMPS OVER THE MOON

...what you have should look something like this

How to use a chisel-edged tool to form letters

The "mystery" of how to make letters thick and thin, and where, is unlocked if the artist understands that the chisel-edged tool, held at one angle to a horizontal line, forms the thick and thin lines in letters.

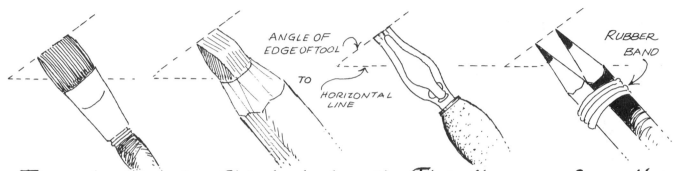

Flat-edged brush   Chisel-edged pencil   Flat-nib pen   2 pencils

The dotted lines above shows the consistent angle to be maintained. The tool is held comfortably in any easy manner. All the tools shown can be used like a chisel-edged tool.

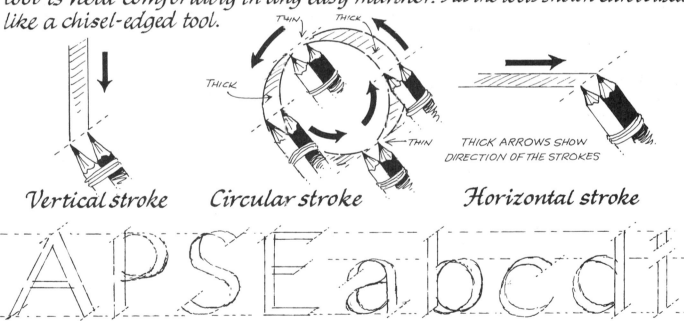

Vertical stroke   Circular stroke   Horizontal stroke

Following simple letter forms, and holding the tool's edge at the same angle as demonstrated above, practice drawing the letters. Forms can be "finished off" later with a single pointed pencil or other tool. Serifs, if wanted, can be added in the same way.

How to write calligraphy

There have been many books written on calligraphy – its histori-
cal development, how-to, etc. The remarks below are very basic,
and the information is presented simply to get someone who
wants to write it started. This is only one form. It has many
variations. To do it reasonably well is self-motivating, and anyone with a real <u>desire</u> to write it <u>can</u>.

ASCENDER →

DESCENDER →

45°

9°

The height of the capitals is 7 pen widths.

Main body of small letters (minuscule) is 5 pen widths high. Ascenders and de-scenders are also 5 pen widths.

Edge of pen is held at a 45° angle to the writing line.

Use thin writing ink.

Letters of a word can join.

Slant of letters is 9° (approx-imately).

Maximum and minimum width of line is attained at right angles.

Basic letter form and same form written with a flat pen.

There is a generally condensed, packed feeling to the lettering. Do not make the letters wide – they will look awkward.

abcdefghijklmnopqrstuv

wxyz

Practice!
Practice!
Practice!

6 AND 8 AND SOMETIMES 2 ARE ABOVE TOP ALIGNING LINE.

1234567890

3, 5, 7, AND 9 ARE BELOW THE BASE LINE.

ABCCDEFGHIJKLMN
OPQRSTUVWXYYYZ

Basic calligraphic forms for capitals. When the situation permits, capitals can have flourishes but not too many in a phrase. The beginning and the end of a sentence are where the flourishes are used most frequently.

The quick brown fox jumps over the.

PENS OR PENCILS
ARE SECURED
TOGETHER.

You can build up interesting letters with 2 pencils or pens held so that an imaginary line joining their points would be at a 45° angle to the aligning line.

SKETCH   SKETCH REFINED   FILLED IN AND RETOUCHED

With some retouching and filling in beautiful calligraphic-type letters are possible, as in the example of the minuscule g to the left.

103

How to use swash letters in design

Swashes are the flourished parts of letters and are used mostly at the beginning or ending of a word or phrase.

A E N e e h n

The letters sketched above are swash letters. They are used to add a note of decoration to an otherwise plain phrase as in the example below.

The quick brown

NORMAN
123
Clothes

They add a note of distinction, if used properly, to a logotype or trade mark.

NORMAN

If you use too many, they may not communicate the message quickly. One or two letters are most effective.

Never use them in the middle of a word or phra

How to letter single stroke letters with a B speedball pen

Below is a demonstration of how to letter single-stroke vertical letters using a B Speedball pen. The light line boxes around the capital letters show the width of the letter in relation to a square. The numbers and arrows show the sequence and direction of strokes.

With the exception of "one," all numbers are almost the same width.

Not a circle

Height of body of lowercase is 2/3 of height of capitals.

How to use an old ruling pen to letter

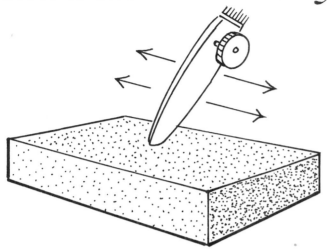

An old ruling pen can be ground down on a sharpening stone to get an edge like this

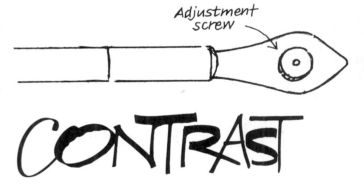

The pen can be dipped directly into ink and used as a writing pen. Keep the slant the same for most of the lettering, changing only for cross-bars on a t, for example. Again, as in brush lettering, practice, practice, practice and you should eventually develop a personal style.

Friends

Custom-made ruling pens with large heads are also available. Varying the angle at which the pen is held as well as the position of your arm can lead to surprising results. The ruling pen can create both broad strokes and thin hairlines. It can be pushed or pulled; or rocked from side to side to achieve special effects. Hold the pen like a spackling knife with the butt-end in the palm of the hand and the thumb and index finger along the barrel.

Adjustment screw

CONTRAST

To achieve "roughened" lettering

Roughened or distressed lettering can achieve an antique look. There are several techniques that can be used. The lettering or calligraphy can be written directly onto a rough, coarse surface such as unpressed watercolor paper. To control the degree of roughness vary the amount of pressure on the pen. Roughness inside the letters can be adjusted by changing the thickness of your ink or paint. A thick ink will leave more holes in your letters. The rough edges of the letters can be exaggerated by adding nicks and breaks with white paint. Another method is to rock your pen on one edge, briefly lifting the other edge off the paper. A third approach is to work on smooth paper with a rough surface, such as sandpaper or corrugated cardboard, underneath. You can also work very small — sometimes with a worn-out nib — on vellum-tooth paper and then enlarge the lettering via a photocopier or photostat camera to final size. The enlargement will emphasize the irregularities in your original writing. Finally, spidery or fuzzy edge lettering can be achieved by writing on porous surfaces such as newsprint, paper towels or Japanese sumi paper.

broad-edge pen "rocked" on smooth paper

broad-edged pen on rough watercolor paper

broad-edge pen on vellum bristol; enlarged 200%

flat-edge brush on watercolor paper

How to design an ornamental letter

Ornamental letters are basically letters with decorative effects, as shown below. They should always read, although some letters have historically been difficult to read because of the heavy ornamentation. They are normally used for short words or phrases — if used in excess, they are hard to read because they call attention to themselves and consequently are difficult to comprehend. The usual styles of ornamentation are shown below.

A			
Basic letter	Simple outline	Simple shading and outline	Inline and outline

Decorate around the letter	Decorate within the letter	Distort the form of the basic letter	Decorate half the letter

Add pictorial matter	Form the letter with pictorial illustration	Some letters are decorative as in Spencerian	Combinations of 2 or more of the other ideas

Below are shown some letters as they were developed in the past. Study them to see how the ideas on the other page are exploited. There are many books on decorative and ornamental letters. Study them, then try some of your own. If you are actually going to use one, try to put significant decorative matter on your letter. If you are going to use your letter for a beer ad, for example, the decorative matter may be wheat, malt, barrels, etc.

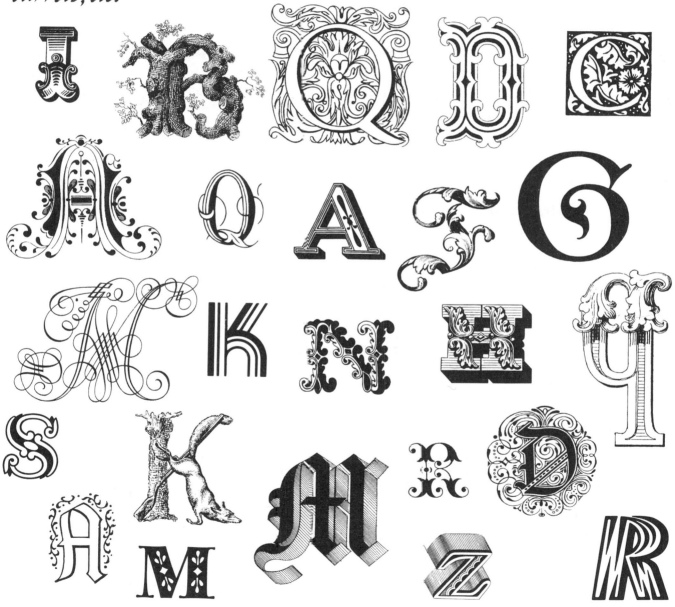

How to relate numbers to caps and lower case

1234567890

These are lining or modern number styles. The upper and lower guide lines contain all the numbers – no parts come above or below.

OPTIONAL

1234567890

These are nonaligning or old-style numbers. Even numbers* extend above the top line. Odd numbers come below the bottom guideline. The numbers 1 and 0 are within the guidelines.

* 4 IS EXCEPTION

SALE

LATEST FROM
~ PARIS ~

15% OFF

JUNIOR MISSES
DRESSES

$89.50

When _applicable_ in _your_ designs, try to relate old-style numbers with lower-case letters and modern numbers with capitals – there is an affinity of old style with lowercase (up and down) and modern numbers with all caps as is obvious, in the examples shown here.

Come to ye olde Church Partie on 31st of May at 5678 st NW

For benefit of Children Fund

Numerals
Some information about arabic and roman numerals

Arabic number	Roman equivalent
1	I
2	II
4	IV
5	V
6	VI
7	VII
9	IX
10	X
11	XI
20	XX
30	XXX
40	XL
41	XLI
49	IL
50	L
60	LX
90	XC
100	C
101	CI
150	CL
200	CC
400	CD
500	D
600	DC
900	CM
1000	M
1976	MCMLXXVI
2000	MM
5000	$\overline{V}$
10,000	$\overline{X}$
100,000	$\overline{C}$
1,000,000	$\overline{M}$

The bar above the letters is a part of the symbol.

Nonaligning Numerals
(Old Style)

1 2 3 4 5 6 7 8 9 0

The above line consists of numbers that are "up-and-down", that is, nonaligning; they are the numbers we got from the arabs or moors in Spain. Only "1", "2" and "0" are within the guide lines. The "6" and "8" are above the guide lines while the odd numbers and "4" fall below the base line.

Aligning Numerals
(Modern)

1 2 3 4 5 6 7 8 9 0

The above line of numbers is called aligning numerals because all the numbers fit within the 2 guide lines. With the exception of the number "1", they are the same width. Because of this and because they align, they are conveniently used in columns and in tabular information. For tabular setting the "1" is usually widened with a foot serif.

How to make a word stand out in a composition

While the information below is basic, the suggestions may help the designer to emphasize a word in a line. The information relates to other design elements as well as words. Combinations of two or more of the devices are possible.

THE WORD IS **MUM** AND YOU KNOW IT	THE WORD IS **MUM** AND YOU KNOW IT	THE WORD IS *MUM* AND YOU KNOW IT
Make the word *larger*—the style and alignment is the same.	Make the word **bolder**—everything else is the same.	The word is in italic—everything else is in regular roman.
THE WORD IS <u>MUM</u> AND YOU KNOW IT	THE WORD IS MUM AND YOU KNOW IT	THE WORD IS MUM AND YOU KNOW IT
<u>Underscore</u> the word or phrase.	Make the word a different color	The word is in a different Style of lettering.
THE WORD IS →MUM AND YOU KNOW IT	THE WORD IS MUM AND YOU KNOW IT	THE WORD IS MUM AND YOU KNOW IT
Use a directional device — fingers pointing, arrows, etc.	Isolate the word.	Use a border device or simple outline.

Tips on making an effective poster

The most effective posters are those in which the main element of the design is communicated at a glance. This main feature should dominate the card — everything else is subordinated. Some smaller elements can be larger and bolder than other small elements, depending on where you want emphasis. Tell the reader at a glance, immediately, what your poster is all about.

Color and tone contrast can be used to support the dominance of the main element. Allow comfortable margins — let your information breathe. Do not use ornate, hard-to-read styles of lettering. Make it easy on the reader.

Too many conflicting elements confuse — do not convey the message immediately and are hard to read. The poster to the right is bad because it has these faults. Remember — everything doesn't have to be large to invite readership.

ST. JOHN'S HIGH SCHOOL WILL PRESENT THEIR 197* ANNUAL DANCE "FROLIK" ON SATURDAY EVE NOV 10

MUSIC BY TOOTS TEAGUE AND HIS BAND

· FOOD · FOR EVERY ONE O

FIREWORKS AT MIDNIGHT

THERE WILL BE A DRAWING FOR A CAR

BRING THE WHOLE FAMILY

How to make letters for an effective wall sign

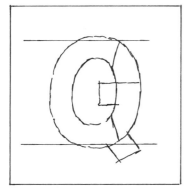

First sketch a basic letter, O, on tracing paper. Use this same letter and sketch the others, C, G, and Q, that are based on the O.

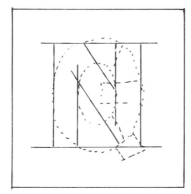

With the first sketch under a new piece of tracing paper, draw the rest of the letters needed for the job.

With a stylus, or a hard pencil, trace the letters on a foil cardboard and then cut them out with a small stencil knife and scissors.

The letters can then be spaced and glued to the wall. Start in the center of your message and work toward either end. The sample below is a copy of a sign that was actually used. The letters, which were 15" high, were pasted onto a white tile wall. The rubber cement which was used was easily cleaned off the wall later.

Having fun with words

A word or words in a caption or logotype or trademark may suggest a treatment which emphasizes the meaning of the word. The examples below show how amusing it can be to use type this way.

ceNsOred

$ue

snuggle

CHAPEL

ejec t

MONA LISA

SKI NG

c()wboy

inc⚬me TAX

about face

PINCH

para=el

L°NELY

PRIS⊗N

ABS NT

STROLL

Question

MARRIAGE

PERI.D

grow

MISTAKE

HꞮDE

CARTOON

DIVO RCE

TRP

ARE YOU AFRAID?

ANGRRRY

T∩NNEL

How to sketch a good letter "S"

Of the 26 letters in the alphabet, "S" is one of the most difficult ones to draw. A few simple suggestions will result in a well-drawn letter that should be acceptable and will have the benefit of being personally created.

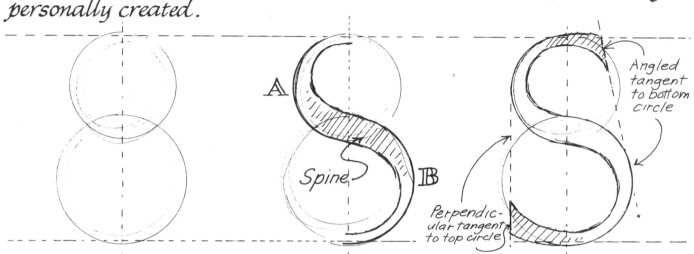

Between 2 guide lines and centered on a perpendicular line, freely sketch 2 slightly overlapping circles. The top circle should be slightly smaller than the bottom circle. Next draw the spine and emphasize the circular parts at A and B. Then form the terminal endings as shown. The terminal at the top right is slanted on a line tangent to the bottom at B; at the bottom left it is perpendicular. All of the curves should flow into each other—without bumps. The serifs can be designed in a variety of ways. As you try other possibilities like the S's shown below, remember that at A and B the form must always be circular, or parts of regular ovals.

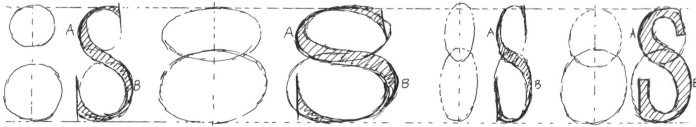

How to indicate small type on a layout

When you squint your eyes and look at a column of type you see lines of body – all lower-case letters have a body, but not all have ascenders and descenders. So the body is what you indicate to give a good impression of the type on a layout.

Sometimes the body is indicated with a solid line and sometimes 2 lines – the top line for the waist line and the bottom line for the base line.

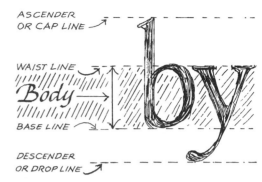

ASCENDER OR CAP LINE

WAIST LINE

Body

BASE LINE

DESCENDER OR DROP LINE

The body of the type – the dark area above – is the part that you indicate.

Single stroke of pencil or other tool

Neat, ruled double lines for each line of type

Scratchy single stroke with breaks here and there

Scratchy double lines broken to indicate words here and there

Wiggly scribbles to simulate words. The squiggles are broken here and there and an aligning line may be indicated.

Nonreading letters (greeking) can be sketched in with aligning waist and base lines. The weight of the type is indicated in the letters.

How to copyfit – from text (manuscript) to type proof

Layout
TEXT

Manuscript
TEXT IS DOUBLE-SPACED
WHEN TYPEWRITTEN.

TYPE
SPECIMENS
ALL STYLES
&
SIZES
ABC Type Co.

**Type
specimen
book**

**Pica
ruler**

TYPE FACES	SIZES				
	10	11	12	14	16
CENTURY EXPANDED	2.6	2.4	2.2	1.8	1.
FUTURA BOOK	3.0	2.7	2.5	2.3	2.
GARAMOND	2.9	2.7	2.6	2.3	2.
NEWS GOTHIC	2.4	2.7	2.3	1.9	2.
TIMES ROMAN	2.8	2.5	2.3	2.1	1.

**Characters-per-pica
chart.** THESE ARE FOUND
IN MOST SPECIMEN BOOKS.

The most accurate system for copyfitting is based on character count.
The following step-by-step sequence is necessary in using this system. The
"tools" you will need are shown above.

(1) Get a total count of all the characters in your manuscript. Count one
each for small letters, word space, and punctuation mark, 2 for each cap.

(2) Select a type style and size from your specimen book.

(3) In picas, measure the width of a line on your layout. Avoid fractions if you can – it will make your arithmetic easier.

(4) Find how many characters of your chosen type face will fit this one
line measure. Calculate it from your characters-per-pica chart.

(5) Divide the number of characters in one line into the total count of
the entire manuscript to find the total number of lines required.

(6) Multiply the number of lines by the point size of your type and you
will get the total depth (in points) for your manuscript.

(7) Add leading (nonprinting space between lines) if desired, and check
the new depth with your layout.

(8) If this final depth doesn't fit your layout, you can change the layout,
or change your type size, or the leading, or all of these, and calculate
the entire program again – until the type fits your layout.

(9) Mark up the manuscript (specs) for the type composition.

• Remember that 12 points = 1 pica, 6 picas = 1 inch, and 72 points = 1 inch.

How and why to copyfit with a computer

The copyfitting process on the previous page is for a manuscript created with a monospaced typewriter. A variable (proportional space) typewriter, word processor or personal computer complicates the procedure. Non-monospaced letters upset the "characters per line × lines × pages" formula. The ability to do tracking (letter spacing) on computers is also a problem. Tracking adjustments render character-per-pica charts useless.* Instead, set a paragraph of the manuscript in your intended font (typeface) at your desired tracking and point size. Then count how many characters you have in an average line (if setting flush left / rag right) or in your intended measure (if setting justified). Continue with the normal procedure, beginning at step ⑤.

You can also treat your computer as a typewriter and create your manuscript in a typewriter font such as Courier. Then you can follow the entire normal copyfitting process. (Remember to leave the tracking at o).

With a computer you can also avoid the entire copyfitting process by adjusting your text on screen as you work. But this is only practical for short texts and those situations where the text has been provided on disk.

When the text is unavailable, unfinished or not yet inputted, copyfitting allows you to estimate the length and dimensions of a printed piece before attempting any typographic work.

*NORMAL (o) TRACKING

Two days after Bull Run, Lincoln penned a memorandum on future Union Strategy. Efforts to make the blockade effective were to be pushed forward;

+20 TRACKING

Two days after Bull Run, Lincoln penned a memorandum on future Union Strategy. Efforts to make the blockade effective

Copy
How to mark up copy for typesetting (composition)

If you don't want to do your own typesetting on the computer you will need to know how to clearly communicate your intentions to the typesetter. Accurate markup of your copy will minimize errors and save both time and money. Use the following procedure.

Paper: Type your copy on 8½" × 11" white bond paper with generous (c. 1") margins. These margins are needed for marking instructions and corrections.

Typing should be clean and _double-spaced_. The copy should be flush left, rag right with only a single space after periods. Indicate emphasis through underlining only. Use Courier or another monospaced typewriter face. Do not "design" the text; your markup does that. Make a backup copy of your text in case the typesetter has questions regarding instructions or content, or the original is lost.

Job number: Proper identification – client, address, phone / fax number, job number, date, etc. should be included on each sheet, preferably at the top.

Numbering. Number sheets at the top in consecutive order. Mark the end of copy on the last sheet.

Corrections should be made above the relevant line in red ink, not pencil. Put instructions in the lefthand margin or at the top of the sheet. See the table of proofreader's marks for the relevant symbols and their proper use.

Never make corrections on the backs of sheets or on Post-It notes or other attached scraps of paper. They may become separated from the copy.

Copyfitting *insures that a given amount of copy will fit into the space planned for it. Use the method given on the next page.*

Markup. *Write your specs at the top of the first sheet or on a separate sheet. Include the name of the typeface, case (capitals, lowercase or small capitals), point size, leading, line length (measure), alignment, paragraph format, use of additional typefaces (including italic and bold), special treatment of type (e.g. drop caps), letterspacing and tracking, etc.*

Nov. 8-11. "Beer Hall Putsch" in Munich, occasioned by the general crisis resulting from the Ruhr occupation and the financial collapse. General Erich Ludendorff and Adolf Hitler, leader of a growing National Socialist Party, attempted to overthrow the Bavarian government. The rising was poorly organized and was easily put down. Hitler was arrested and sentenced to five years in prison. While serving his term he wrote Mein Kampf.

Nov. 8-11. "BEER HALL PUTSCH" in Munich, occasioned by the general crisis resulting from the Ruhr occupation and the financial collapse. General Erich Ludendorff and Adolf Hitler, leader of a growing National Socialist Party, attempted to overthrow the Bavarian government. The rising was poorly organized and was easily put down. Hitler was arrested and sentenced to five years in prison. While serving his term he wrote *Mein Kampf*, a book outlining his career, his theories, and his program.

THE MANUSCRIPT ON THE LEFT IS PROPERLY TYPED AND READY FOR SPECING.

THE MANUSCRIPT ON THE RIGHT HAS BEEN "DESIGNED". THE JUSTIFICATION MAKES IT DIFFICULT TO CAST-OFF OR CHARACTER COUNT. THE SINGLE SPACING LEAVES NO ROOM FOR CORRECTIONS OR SPECS.

How to "spec" (specify) type for the printer

① If you have more than 1 page, number all the pages of your typed manuscript.

② Be sure the copy you give to the printer is letter-perfect — no mistakes.

③ Type all the copy, double spaced, no wider than 5½" and centered on an 8½" x 11" sheet. Use the margins for marking up the copy.

④ Write the date you want the proofs, and how many and what kind you want (repro or RC, laser, film negative, galley or page makeup) at the top of the first page of your manuscript. Also indicate if the final output, if digitally composed, is to be disk or not.

⑤ If you have any question about anything call and ask the typesetter or service bureau.

⑥ Always send a sketch of your type arrangements, from your layout, with your specs to the printer.

⑦ Mark any copy on the manuscript that you do not want set "delete" or DNS ("do not set"). Do this for handlettering, for example.

⑧ Always give the complete names of the typeface styles. (Get them from a type specimen book.)

⑨ Before you send it out, always check your job.

⑩ Write clear, legible instructions.

⑪ Write "The end" on the last page of the manuscript when there is more than one page.

⑫ Sign every sheet (at the bottom) and give your company's name and telephone number.

When you provide a disk for service bureau output check that:

① include all fonts used.

② indicate your page layout program, including version number.

③ indicate the type of output desired.

④ include your name, address, phone and fax numbers.

⑤ provide a hard copy of your text (original manuscript or laser copy).

122

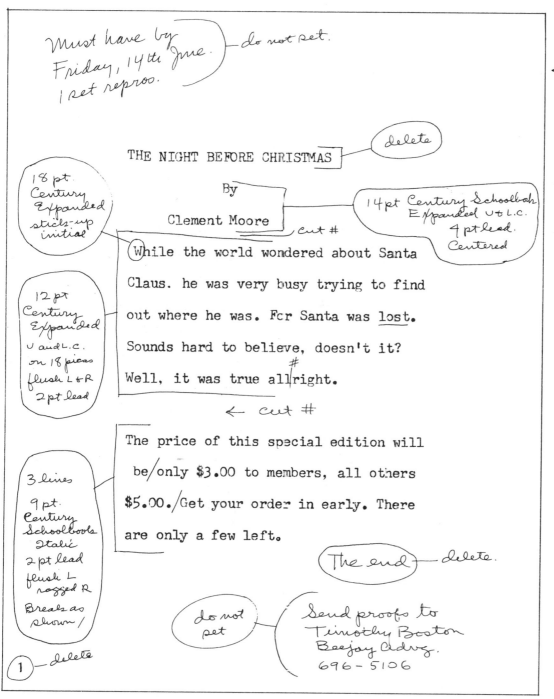

Small scale model of a manuscript sheet, marked up for the printer

(ABOUT 2/3 OF 8½"x11")

Must have by Friday, 14th June. 1 set repros. — do not set.

THE NIGHT BEFORE CHRISTMAS — delete

By

Clement Moore

18 pt. Century Expanded stick-up initial

14 pt Century Schoolbook Expanded U & L.C. 4 pt lead. Centered

cut #

While the world wondered about Santa

Claus. he was very busy trying to find

out where he was. For Santa was lost.

Sounds hard to believe, doesn't it?

Well, it was true all#right.

12 pt Century Expanded U and L.C. on 18 picas flush L & R 2 pt lead

← cut #

The price of this special edition will

be/only $3.00 to members, all others

$5.00./Get your order in early. There

are only a few left.

3 lines 9 pt. Century Schoolbook Italic 2 pt lead flush L ragged R Breaks as shown /

The end — delete.

do not set

Send proofs to Timothy Boston Beejay Bldg. 696-5106

1 — delete

Do not be too wordy. However, if some unusual effect is desired, describe it as simply and clearly as you can. If it is too complicated, call the printer, or have him call you when he gets your specs.

```
|<--------- 40 characters --------->|
Then suddenly, out of the storm there appeared... a reindeer!

It leaped and pranced about in the snow. Reindeer just LOVE

snow, you know. Santa took some food out of his sleigh

and held it out to the reindeer. It stopped prancing and

shyly approached.
```

Let's take the layout shown at the top of the opposite page in miniature and size it for the printer. We pick 12 pt. Century Expanded for our type. By consulting the characters-per-pica chart we find that there are 2.2 characters of this type in 1 pica. By actual measurement on our layout, the length of the lines (measure) is 18 picas. So there are 40 characters (approx.) of this type in 18 picas (2.2 x 18 = 39.6 or 40 characters). Count over 40 characters (including word spaces and punctuation marks) on the manuscript and mark it. Draw a perpendicular line through this mark as shown above. There are 4 full lines of text to the left of this line. Count the characters to the right of the vertical line, add the characters of the last 2 words, and divide the total by 40. This gives us 3 lines, and added to the 4 we have a total of 7 lines. We feel we need 2 pts. of leading between the lines. You can now calculate the total depth the type will be. If this depth checks with your layout, spec the manuscript and order the type. Proofread the proofs when they come back and if they are perfect, paste them in position on your mechanical.

The Reproduction Proof

Then suddenly, out of the storm there appeared...a reindeer! It leaped and pranced about in the snow. Reindeer just LOVE snow, you know. Santa took some food out of his sleigh and held it out to the reindeer. It stopped prancing and shyly approached.

Length-of-line and leading tables

A beginner designing typographic text copy should adhere to time-tested rules for length of line and leading (the space between lines) in order to achieve maximum readability of the text — which is, after all, the primary aim of all good typography. Shown below are accepted standards for accomplishing this maximum legibility. As the designer's experience widens he may vary these requirements for artistic effect, but this does not alter the legibility rules.

Length-of-line table

TYPE SIZE	MINIMUM LENGTH	MAXIMUM LENGTH
6 point	8 picas	10 picas
8 "	9 "	13 "
10 "	13 "	16 "
11 "	13 "	18 "
12 "	14 "	21 "
14 "	18 "	24 "
18 "	24 "	30 "

Leading table

TYPE SIZE	MINIMUM LEADING	MAXIMUM LEADING
6 point	Solid (no lead)	1 point
8 "	"	2 "
10 "	Solid to 2 point	4 "
11 "	1 point	4 "
12 "	2 "	6 "
14 "	3 "	8 "

Since there are 72 points to 1 inch and 6 picas to 1 inch, therefore 12 points equal 1 pica. For type sizes larger than those given, use your own judgment.

How to make a scale for character counting when "specing" type

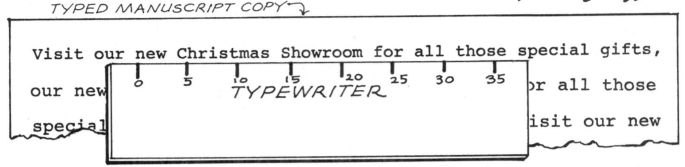

Visit our new Christmas Showroom for all those special gifts,

our new [TYPEWRITER scale: 0 5 10 15 20 25 30 35] or all those

special isit our new

On a piece of card (5"x 2" or any size you need) mark off on one side, in divisions of 5, the character count of the manuscript copy in typewriter type (e.g. Courier). Lay the edge of the card parallel to the typewritten copy to count the characters. Label it "TYPEWRITER."

PAGE FROM TYPE SPECIMEN BOOK

CONSORT LIGHT

18 Point (Foundry)

Our alphabet, borrowed from the Romans, who

AB [TYPE STYLE scale: 0 5 10 15 20 25 30] VXYZ $12

24 Point

Ou [TYPEWRITER scale: 35 30 25 20 15 10 5 0] he Roma

ABCDEFGHIJKLMNOPQRSTUVWX

Turn the card around and mark the other edge with the character count of the type you have selected for your layout. Mark this side "TYPE STYLE." You can now easily manipulate this card on your layout (to check how many characters of the type will fall on a line) with the character count on your typewritten copy. When using a word processing program be sure to maintain the same kerning and tracking values throughout a document.

126

How to proofread printed copy

Shown below are standard proofreader's marks, what they mean, and an example of each. They should be learned and used by all who handle type proofs.

MARK	EXPLANATION	EXAMPLE
ℓ	TAKE OUT CHARACTER	ℓ The caffrd
∧	LEFT OUT, INSERT	h Te card
#	INSERT SPACE	# Thecard
∨	SUPERSCRIPT	∨ The card
eq#	EVEN SPACE	eq# The black card
⌣	LESS SPACE	⌣ The card
⌒	CLOSE UP; NO SPACE	⌒ The ca rd
tr	TRANSPOSE	tr The card red
wf	WRONG FONT	wf The card
lc	LOWER CASE	lc The Card
sc	SMALL CAPS	sc The card
c+sc	CAPITALS AND SMALL CAPS.	c+sc The card
caps	CAPITALS	caps The card
A̲	CAPITALIZE	C The card
ital	ITALIC	ital The card
rom	ROMAN	rom The card
bf	BOLD FACE	bf The card
stet	LET IT STAND	stet The card
out sc	OUT, SEE COPY	out sc He card
spell out	SPELL OUT	spell out King Geo.
¶	START PARAGRAPH	¶ out. The card
⌐	BASELINE SHIFT (UP)	⌐ The card
⌐	BASELINE SHIFT (DOWN)	⌐ The card
⊏	MOVE LEFT	⊏ The card
⊐	MOVE RIGHT	⊐ The card
‖	ALIGN TYPE	‖ The card / Ace of spa
=	STRAIGHTEN LINE	= The card
⊙	INSERT PERIOD	⊙ The card
⸲/	INSERT COMMA	⸲/ The card
:/	INSERT COLON	:/ The card
⸴/	INSERT SEMICOLON	⸴/ The card
⸲	INSERT APOSTROPHE	⸲ The boys card
⸲⸲	INSERT QUOTATION MARKS	⸲⸲ Make it card
=/	INSERT HYPHEN	=/ A card mark
!	INSERT EXCLAMATION MARK	! What a card
?	INSERT QUESTION MARK	? Whose card
⓺	QUERY FOR AUTHOR	⓺ is The card dealt
[/]	INSERT BRACKETS	[/] The ace card
(/)	INSERT PARENTHESES	(/) The card 1
|1/N|	INSERT 1-EN DASH	|1/N| The card
|1/M|	INSERT 1-EM DASH	|1/M| The card
|2/M|	INSERT 2-EM DASH	|2/M| The card
▫	INDENT 1-EM	▫ The card
▭	INDENT 2-EMS	▭ The card
ld>	INSERT LEAD BETWEEN LINES	ld> The card was dealt by Hal
hr#	INSERT HAIR SPACE	hr# The card was
ℓ	DELETE AND CLOSE UP	ℓ The boys card
Qu?	IS THIS RIGHT?	Qu? The red card

127

The best time to correct or edit copy is before it leaves your hand for the typesetter or formatter. When correcting proofs use red ink to clearly show the errors. Make all the corrections in the margins of the proof. Strike a vertical or diagonal line through a wrong letter and a horizontal line with a "pig's tail" through a wrong word or sentence. Shown below is a corrected proof.

It does not appear that the earliest printers had any method of correcting errors before the form was on the press/ The learned The learned correctors of the first two centuries of printing were not proof/readers in our sense, they were rather what we should term office editors. Their labors were chiefly to see that the proof corresponded to the copy, but that the printed page was correct in its latinity / that the words were there, and that the sense was right. They cared but little about orthography, bad letters or purely printers errors, and when the text seemed to them wrong they consulted fresh authorities or altered it on their own responsibility. Good proofs, in the modern sense, were impossible until professional readers were employed / men who had first a printer's education, and then spent many years in the correcion of proof. The orthography of English, which for the past century has undergone little change, was very fluctuating until after the publication of Johnson's Dictionary, and capitals, which have been used with considerable regularity for the past 80 years, were previously used on the miss or hit plan. The approach to regularity, so far as we have, may be attributed to the growth of a class of professional proof readers, and it is to them that we owe the correctness of modern printing. More er/ors have been found in the Bible than in any other one work. For many generations it was frequently the case that Bibles were brought out stealthily, from fear of governmental interference. They were frequently printed from imperfect texts, and were often modified to meet the views of those who publised them. The story is related that a certain woman in Germany, who was the wife of a Printer, and had become disgusted with the continual assertions of the superiority of man over woman which she had heard, hurried into the composing room while her husband was at supper and altered a sentence in the Bible, which he was printing, so that it read Narr instead of Herr, thus making the verse read "And he shall be thy fool" instead of "and he shall be thy lord." The word not was omitted by Barker, the King's printer in

How to make your own typeface

First design your alphabet, including all necessary figures and punctuation. Be sure to draw guidelines to indicate the baseline of your letters. Next make a master photostat of your alphabet. Then, when you need your alphabet for a design you can make new photostats from the master. Cut out the letters you need (if you need more than one copy of a letter, two e s for instance, you will have to make several photostats), assemble them with proper spacing, paste them down, and then reshoot to final size. (Remember to white-out the guidelines). _Never_ cut up your master sheet.

With the increased presence of computers there is now another, more flexible, alternative for making your own typefaces. Three software programs — Fontographer, Font Studio, and Ikarus-M — are available for creating digital fonts with your computer. Fontographer is the most popular and is available for both Windows and Macintosh environments. Font Studio is used by several professionals, but suffers from a lack of recent upgrades. Finally, Ikarus-M is a simpler version of the professional Ikarus program used by large type foundries. Fontographer and Font Studio use Bezier curves to create outlines. Ikarus simply connects the dots of an outline. It is more precise, yet more time-consuming and inflexible.

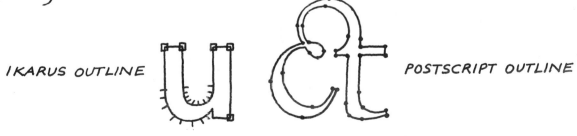

IKARUS OUTLINE   POSTSCRIPT OUTLINE

129

Designing an alphabet

When making your own alphabet don't start by designing from A to Z. Group the letters of the alphabet into families. Design key letters for each family first. For instance, a popular keyword among type designers is "Hamburgefonts". The letters contained in this word are all different. The **H** provides capital height; the **b** & **f** provide ascender height; the **t** is frequently a unique height between ascender and x-height; **a, e, m, n, o, r, u** and **s** provide x-height; and **g** provides descender depth. Difficult and highly distinctive letters like **a, g** and **s** are present along with normal letters such as **m** and **o**. Family groups vary from alphabet to alphabet, but here is a basic grouping derived from shape (not proportion):

Capital letters

Round	**O Q C G**
Semi-round	**D B R P S**
Rectangular	**E F L H T I**
Curved	**J U**
Angular	**A V W X Y Z**
	K M N

Lowercase letters

Round	**o c e s g**
Semi-round	**b d p q**
Arched	**h n m u a**
Curved	**r j f t**
Angular	**v w x y k z**
Vertical	**i l**

capital height ⟶ Ascender height ⟶ x-height

Hamburgefonts

Descender depth

How to use transfer sheets and letters

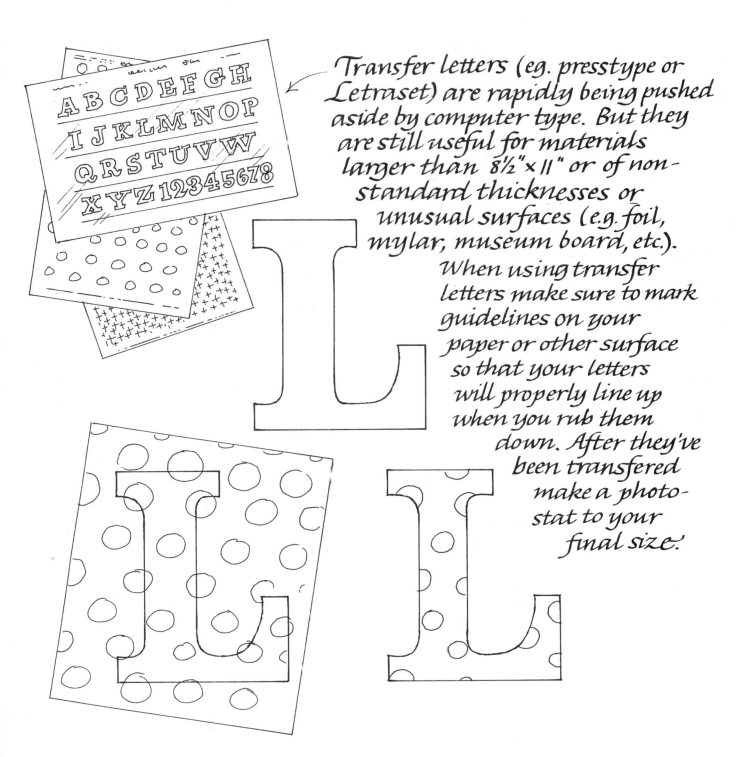

Transfer letters (eg. presstype or Letraset) are rapidly being pushed aside by computer type. But they are still useful for materials larger than 8½"×11" or of non-standard thicknesses or unusual surfaces (e.g. foil, mylar, museum board, etc.).

When using transfer letters make sure to mark guidelines on your paper or other surface so that your letters will properly line up when you rub them down. After they've been transfered make a photo-stat to your final size!

Design and Layout
How to use graph paper as an aid in design

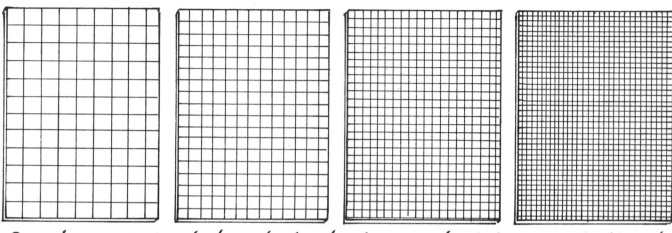

Graph paper can be bought in sheets or pads. It is usually lined with blue lines, will not reproduce if line art (black) is drawn on the graph paper. It comes in many sizes (squares per inch) and can be used for a variety of sized layouts scaled to the sizes of the squares. The paper usually takes writing ink well and thus is good for calligraphy to be reproduced – the blue lines acting as guide lines.

The quick bro
www'wn fox
jumped overrr
the lazy dog
aadddggggg
The quick 12345
Dennis Park.k

It is great for practicing calligraphy and is inexpensive. It can also be used under tissue or vellum sheets to help align elements of a layout. It can be "positioned" in many angles and taped to sheet underneath.

GRAPH PAPER

TRACING PAD

How to achieve order in a design

Here are only a few ways that the graphic designer can achieve order in his layouts.

> **A CAT NAMED PI**
> Once upon a time, in a lone little village at

Keep the caption and text style the same. You achieve unity of type most effectively in this way.

Coach	FERD SONDERN
Mr. Simsi	GEORGE PORTER
Siss	LILI GAYDOS
Chairman	STEPHANIE HARRIS
Sammy	HAL GREER

Common alignments give unity to an arrangement.

The left edge of the type "follows" the illustration's irregular edge.

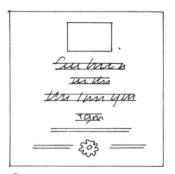

Center all elements for a *symmetric* balance. Lines arranged in this manner have great unity.

In this example of *asymmetric* balance, the large gray area at the top left balances the small black element on the lower right.

The 2 most common methods to have type set for a neat and unified look are shown below.

Flush left and right type lines.

Flush left type lines with ragged right. Flush right and ragged left is not used often.

How to make a device for visualizing your layout

When you are making a layout on a larger (than layout) pad, visualizing what your layout really looks like can be deceptive (because of the surrounding white space). To help you visualize completely what your trimmed layout will look like when it is printed use the device shown below.

The white space around is like a mat on a framed watercolor. It has a tendency to make your layout look better than it is

Cut 2 large, wide black cardboard pieces as shown on the upper right. Use them as shown here. You may want to make some changes.

LAYOUT

L-SHAPES ARE MADE AS WIDE AND LONG AS YOUR USUAL LAYOUT SIZES.

How to visualize a design on different backgrounds

In developing a design it is sometimes difficult to imagine what your design will look like against various backgrounds. If the design is in one color or more and in line, follow the directions below.

A LITTLE SOAP, SALIVA, OR NONCRAWL CAN BE ADDED TO PAINT TO AID IN ADHERING IT TO ACETATE.

ACETATE

This is your design. Attach it to drawing board, lay a piece of acetate over it, and redraw the design. It doesn't have to be finished art—just enough to represent your design. This acetate drawing can now be laid over different colored backgrounds and patterns so you can evaluate them and reach a decision.

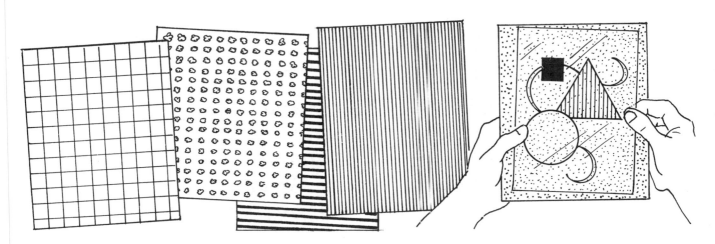

How to make an aid for drawing repeated layouts

Suppose you have many layouts like the one on the left to lay out in pencil. Instead of measuring each one separately use the method below to save you much time.

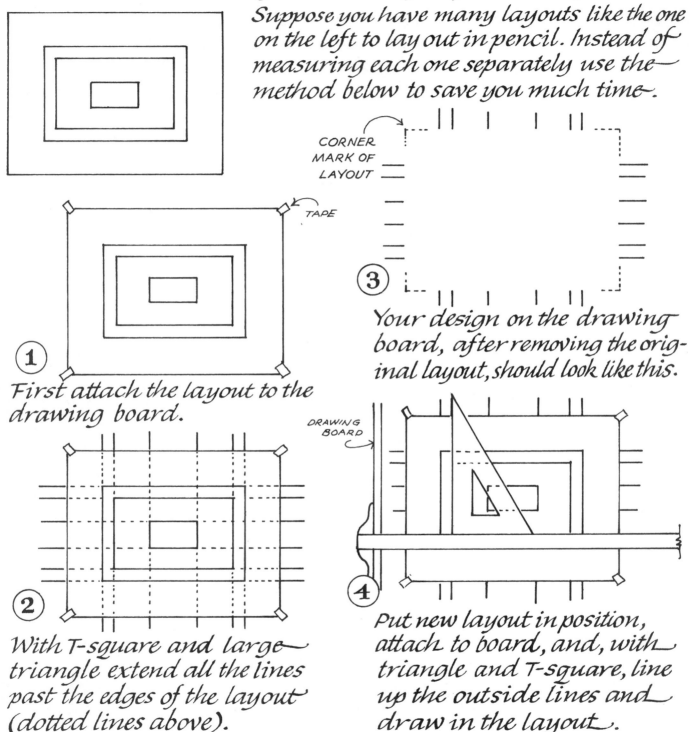

CORNER MARK OF LAYOUT

TAPE

① First attach the layout to the drawing board.

② With T-square and large triangle extend all the lines past the edges of the layout (dotted lines above).

③ Your design on the drawing board, after removing the original layout, should look like this.

DRAWING BOARD

④ Put new layout in position, attach to board, and, with triangle and T-square, line up the outside lines and draw in the layout.

How to place images under a layout for tracing

You may have a layout taped to a drawing board and do not want to lift it in order to trace photos or other images. The following aid may help you solve this problem.

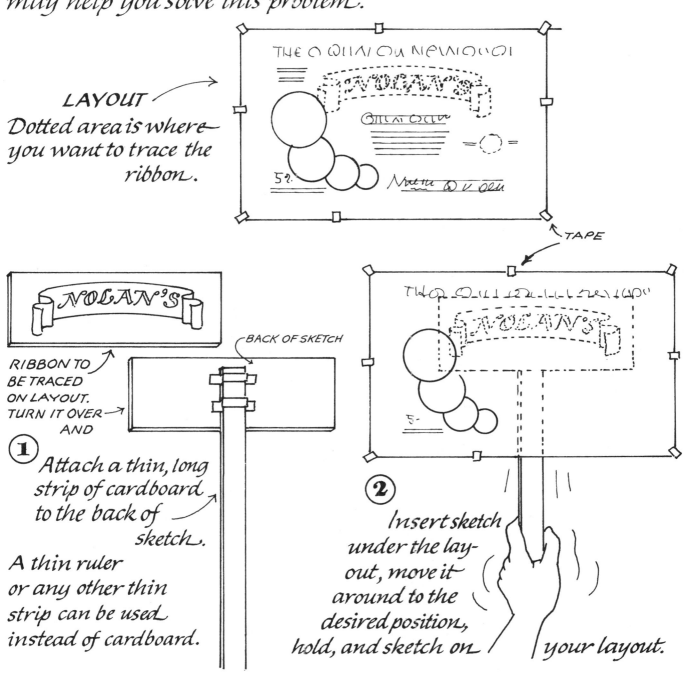

LAYOUT — Dotted area is where you want to trace the ribbon.

TAPE

RIBBON TO BE TRACED ON LAYOUT. TURN IT OVER AND

BACK OF SKETCH

① Attach a thin, long strip of cardboard to the back of sketch.

A thin ruler or any other thin strip can be used instead of cardboard.

② Insert sketch under the layout, move it around to the desired position, hold, and sketch on your layout.

How to make a transfer sheet

Rolls of transfer sheets for any purpose can be bought in art stores but they are a little expensive for modest budgets. Here's how you can make your own — for any purpose.

① On a piece of tracing paper use the side of a soft pencil and rub the entire surface in one direction.

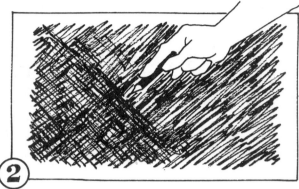

② Now rub the entire surface in the opposite direction.

③ Rub the entire area with your finger or a cotton ball.

④ A slightly damp cotton ball with a drop of rubber cement thinner can be rubbed over the area after ③ and, starting at ①, repeat all steps.

A hard-pointed 5H or 6H pencil should be used to transfer the image, with the transfer sheet between. Stabilo pencils (all colors) can be used to make transfer sheets to transfer images onto glass or glossy photos. Colored pastels can also be used instead of graphite pencils.

How to make a blue transfer sheet for pencil designs

Suppose you made a pencil drawing on a piece of tracing paper and now want to transfer the image to illustration board for making a final finished drawing. Instead of making a gray-pencil transfer sheet (the gray pencil lines are difficult to see), use a blue pastel for the sheet and you will then see the pencil lines more clearly as you trace the drawing.

First, apply pastel to a separate tracing sheet. Then spread the ↗

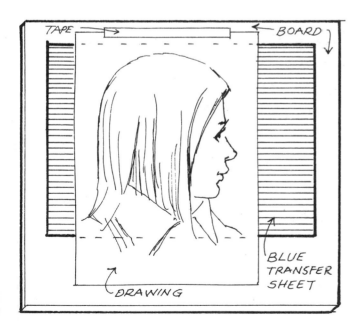

pastel with rubber cement thinner and a small cotton ball. Repeat this procedure several times. Tape the drawing to the board and slip the blue transfer sheet, face down, between it and the board. <u>You will see the pencil lines</u> of the <u>drawing clearly</u>. Trace the drawing, transferring the image to the board. When you are finished, remove the tracing paper and also the drawing on top of the illustration board.

Some notes on color

Volumes have been written on color. Here are a few basic principles.

<u>Warm</u> <u>colors</u> are yellow, orange, and red. They are positive and aggressive, restless and stimulating.

<u>Cool</u> <u>colors</u> are blues, greens, and violets. They are negative and retiring, tranquil and serene.

<u>Color preferences</u> of most people are pure colors in the following order: ① Red, ② Blue, ③ Violet, ④ Green, ⑤ Orange, and ⑥ Yellow.

<u>To deepen, soften, or tone</u> a color, add a little of its complement. For example, a touch of green added to red will deepen or darken the red.

<u>Color mixing.</u> Orange with a touch of ultramarine makes terra-cotta. Yellow with a bit of violet makes olive. Green with a bit of magenta makes myrtle. Turquoise with a touch of red makes peacock blue. Violet with a bit of yellow makes plum. Ultramarine with a touch of orange makes navy blue. Magenta with a bit of green makes claret. Magenta and ultramarine make a great purple, but don't mix ultramarine with vermillion — a muddy and dirty purple. Try not to use black to deepen a color or white to lighten it. Use lighter or darker colors instead.

<u>Colors' "other names".</u> If you don't know what it is, you may find it here:

Pale green – seafoam
Dark green – bottle green, forest gr'n.
Olive green – emerald green
Dark blue – midnight, gulf, navy
Pea green – tropical green, oriental green
Pale blue – robin's egg
Navy blue – marine blue
Ultramarine – new blue
Yellow – canary, buttercup

Corn – light orange, Persian orange
Orange – tangerine
Dark brown – beaver, cocoa
Tan – buff
Fawn – light brown, sepia
Salmon – coral
Maroon – oxblood
Pale gray – pearl gray
Shetland green – dark green

140

How to use a straight edge for drawing lines

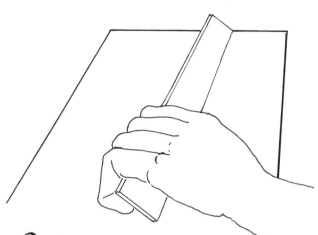

Position of the left hand holding the ruler. The finger-tips are on the drawing surface.

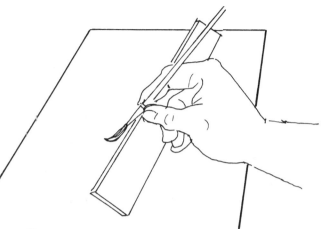

Position of the right hand holding the brush against the ruler.

A pen, brush, or other tool can be used expediently against a ruler for drawing straight lines as shown.

The ruler is held rigidly on the drawing surface by the left hand.

The brush is held against the edge of the ruler and drawn from left to right.

Practice this and it will soon be an easy operation.

Practice spread, dotted, and other lines.

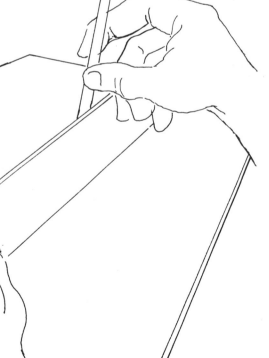

How to draw expedient parallel lines

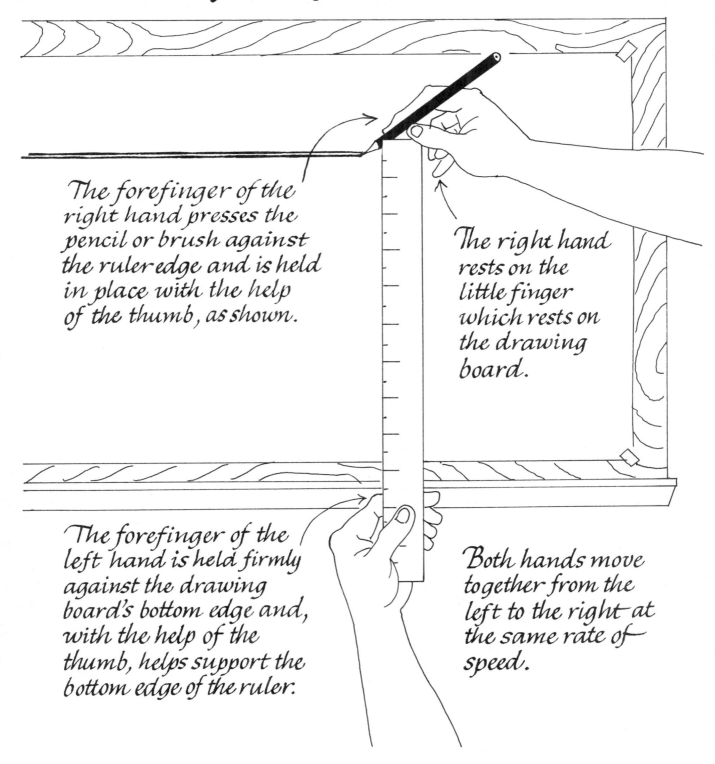

The forefinger of the right hand presses the pencil or brush against the ruler edge and is held in place with the help of the thumb, as shown.

The right hand rests on the little finger which rests on the drawing board.

The forefinger of the left hand is held firmly against the drawing board's bottom edge and, with the help of the thumb, helps support the bottom edge of the ruler.

Both hands move together from the left to the right at the same rate of speed.

142

How to make a template for dotted lines

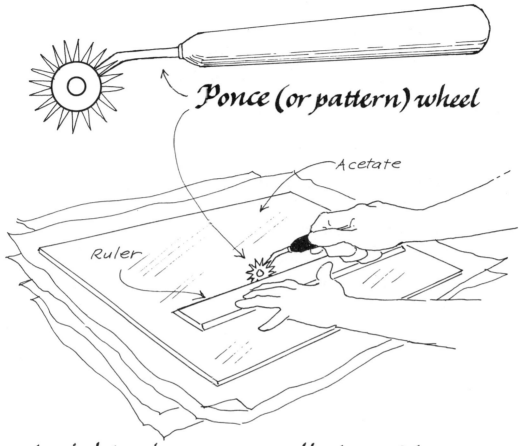

Ponce (or pattern) wheel

Acetate

Ruler

Lay a straight edge on a small piece of heavy acetate. The acetate rests on a soft backing like a large blotter or a folded newspaper. Rule a line of holes with the ponce wheel, impressing the regularly spaced holes into the acetate. Turn the acetate over and sandpaper the holes.

The template can now be used, with a wad of color, to make dotted lines on art or anywhere else.

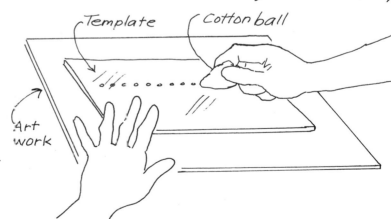

Template   Cotton ball

Art work

How to mark a point without measuring

Suppose you have a type proof that you want to be sure fits a certain area on an already partly designed layout. You want to check certain points of the type with similar points on your layout.

Hold the proof in the position you want over the layout. Hold a pencil or some other pointer with the other hand, the butt of the hand resting firmly on the drawing board and the pointer touching the type's margin. Pull the proof away but do not move the marker. Your mark is now established on the layout.

The type proof

The same method can be used for marking points in other situations.

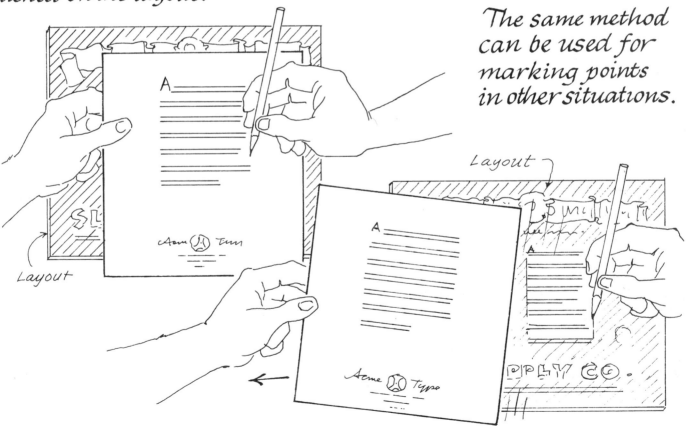

Layout

Layout

Measuring Tricks
How to find the center between two points quickly

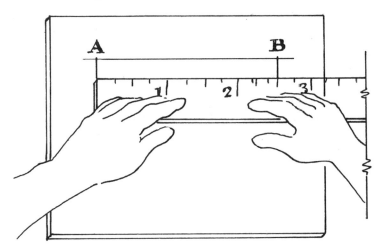

Suppose that you wanted to find the center between points A and B on the sketch to the left. Instead of putting the zero of your ruler at point A, and measuring the actual distance to B, and then dividing it, which gets involved with fractions, do this ↴

Move your ruler left and right until you get a convenient equal distance between numbers (in inches). For example, the ruler measures exactly ¼" from the 1" mark to the left and ¼" from the 3" mark to the right so that the 2" mark would be the center.

With a little practice this method will save you a lot of time.

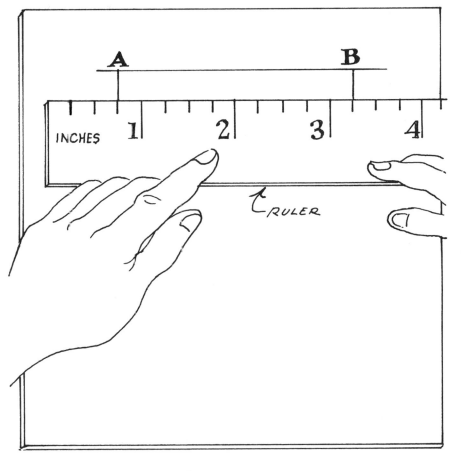

How to divide any line into equal parts without a ruler

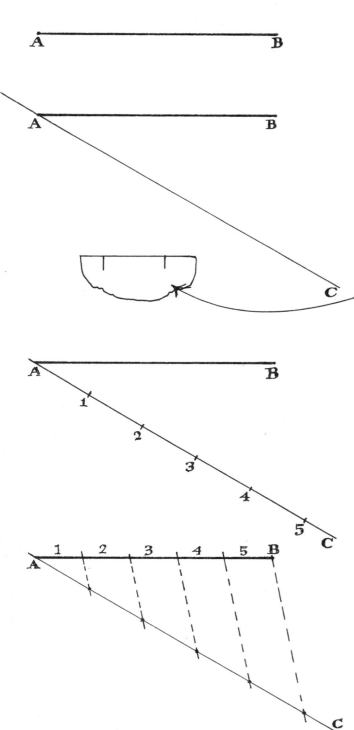

Let the line which we wish to divide into five equal parts be AB.

Construct a line through A to any distance. This line is marked AC and is at any angle to AB.

On a straight-edge piece of paper mark any distance with two marks. This is your marking piece.

Using this marking piece, measure off the desired number of divisions (e.g., 5 here). You do not have to meet C — AC is just an arbitrary line.

Turn the paper so that the 5th mark and B line up on your T square. As you draw parallel lines for all the marks, you divide AB into 5 equal parts (where the lines cross).

How to divide any distance between lines into any number of equal spaces

In the diagram below let AB and CD be the parallel lines, and AC or BD the distance...

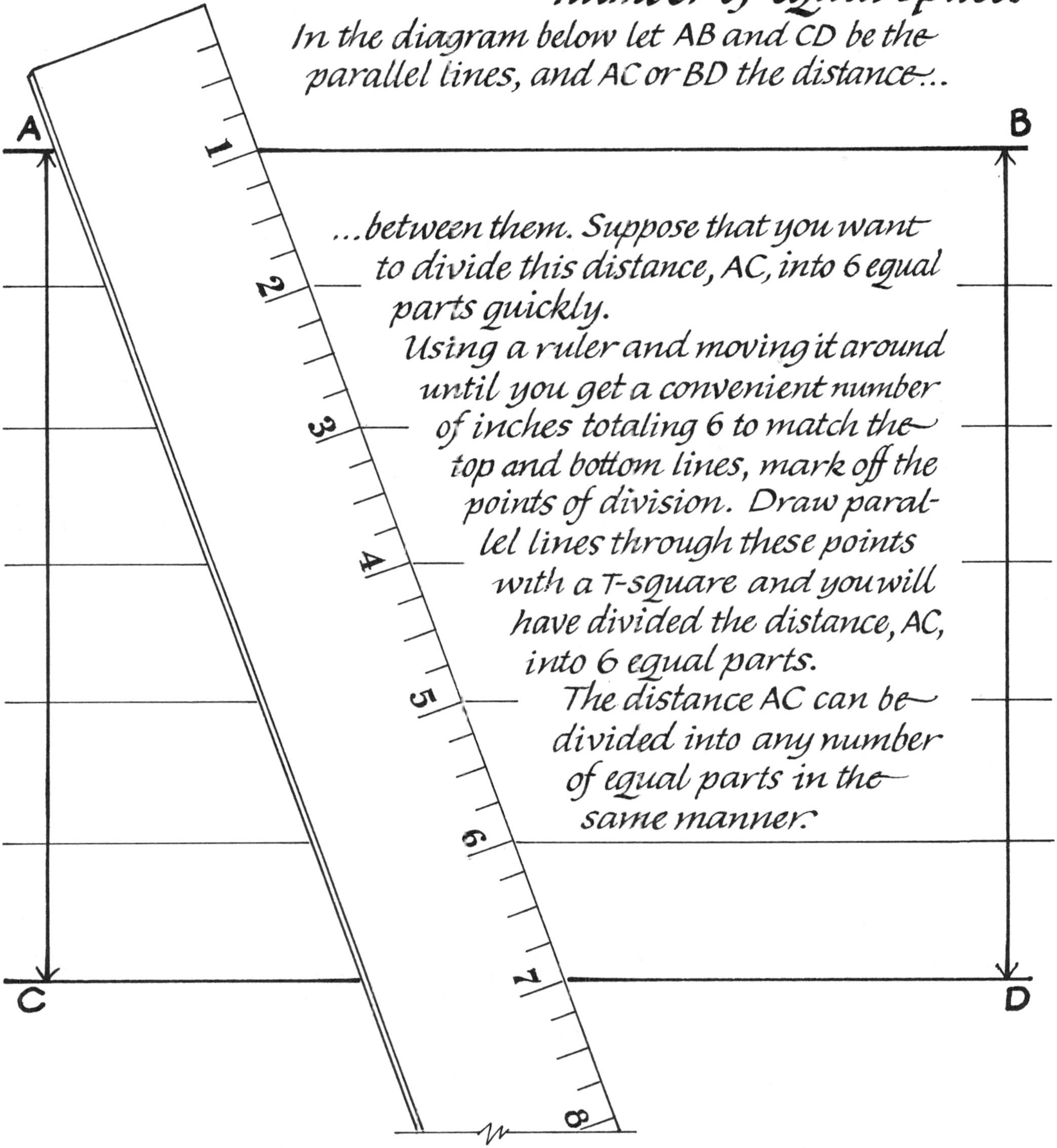

...between them. Suppose that you want to divide this distance, AC, into 6 equal parts quickly.

Using a ruler and moving it around until you get a convenient number of inches totaling 6 to match the top and bottom lines, mark off the points of division. Draw parallel lines through these points with a T-square and you will have divided the distance, AC, into 6 equal parts.

The distance AC can be divided into any number of equal parts in the same manner.

How to make a proportional scaling device

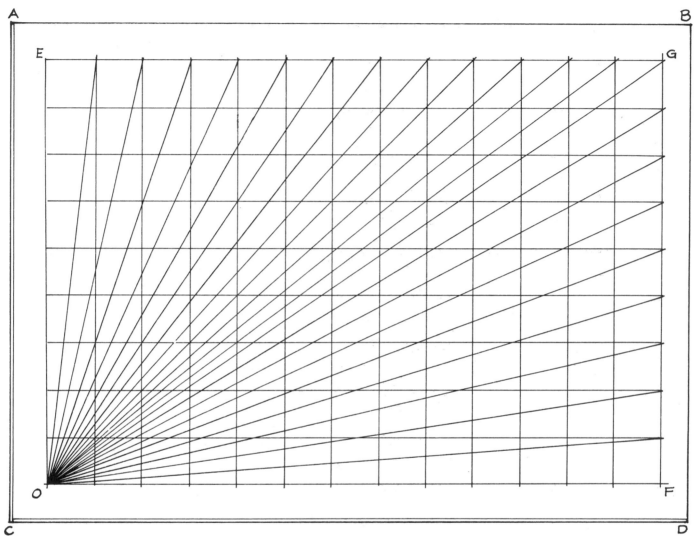

On a piece of acetate (ABCD), draw the left-hand vertical line, OE, and at a right angle to it draw the horizontal line, OF. Divide these lines into any equal number of equal dimensions and draw the grid, OFGE. From O, construct diagonals to these outside points and draw the radiating lines. By laying this device over a small rectangle, you can mark off any enlargement desired. It can also be used for making reductions.

How to enlarge elements on a design proportionately

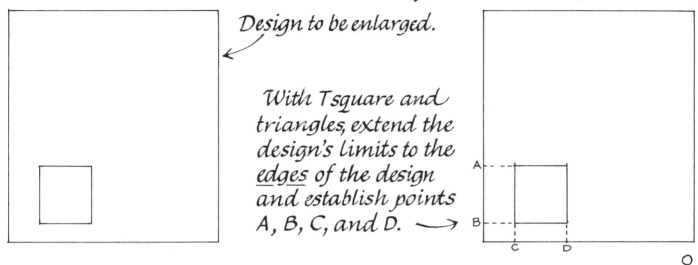

Design to be enlarged.

With Tsquare and triangles, extend the design's limits to the *edges* of the design and establish points A, B, C, and D. ➝

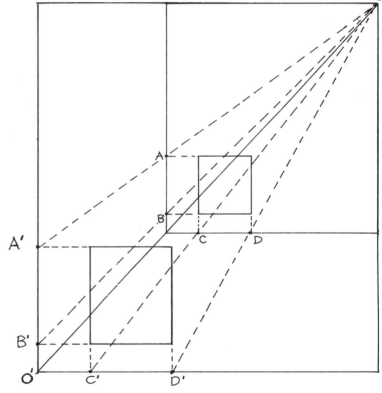

Begin to enlarge the design by drawing a diagonal from corner O and establishing O' on the design at the bottom. With O as the radiating point, extend and draw lines OA to OA', OB to OB', OC to OC' and OD to OD'. From points A' and B' draw parallel lines across the new design, and from points C' and D' erect perpendicular lines. As these lines intersect, they form the enlarged rectangle, which is in exact proportion to the smaller design at top left of this page.

Limits of an irregular area can be extended proportionally in a similar fashion.

How to enlarge images by the squares method

If you have a photo, layout, or drawing that you want to enlarge and no other convenient method of enlarging is available, such as a photostat machine, the method below is one way to obtain a reasonable enlargement.

TISSUE PAPER

① Attach tissue paper to the image and trace it carefully. Divide the area into any number of squares.

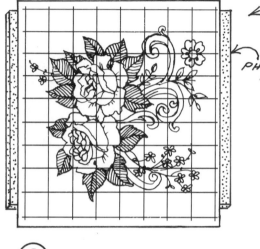

PHOTO OR DRAWING

②

On a larger piece of tissue paper or board repeat the number of squares on the smaller sketch. These squares will be much larger. Carefully draw in corresponding squares exactly what is in the small sketch.

You can number the squares if you wish. The finish may not be an exact enlargement — that depends on how carefully you duplicate the squares.

Forming Circles, Ovals, and Spirals
How to draw a circle with no visible center mark

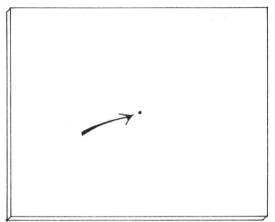

① With a pencil, determine exactly where the center of the circle will be on the art.

② Cut a small square out of illustration board and rubber cement it over the center of the circle.

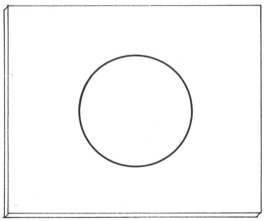

③ Draw a circle with an ink or pencil compass.

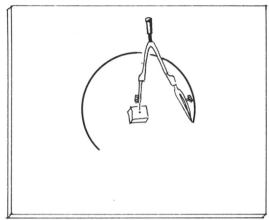

④ After you remove the center card and clean away the rubber cement, you are left with a circle that has no visible center mark.

Apply this method in other instances where pinprick holes on the art are to be avoided.

How to find the center of any circle

A chord is a straight line that cuts through any part of a circle at 2 points. Suppose that you have a circle and want to find the center of it.

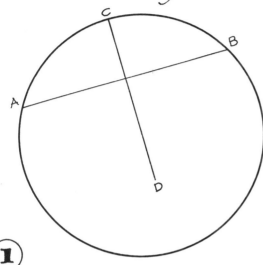

① First draw a chord (AB), divide it in half, and draw a perpendicular line (CD) through this center, as above.

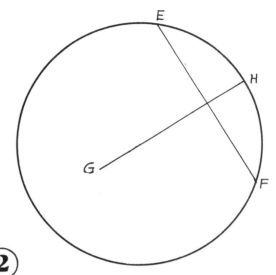

② Draw any other chord (EF) on the same circle, as above. Find the center of this chord and draw a perpendicular line (GH)

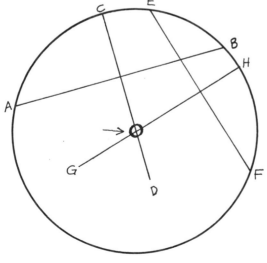

③ Where these two perpendiculars, CD and GH, intersect is the center of the circle (O).

How to draw a circle through any three points not on a straight line

1
Suppose you have 3 points not on a straight line and want to draw a circle through them.

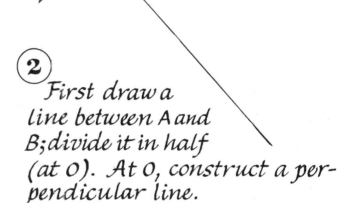

2
First draw a line between A and B; divide it in half (at O). At O, construct a perpendicular line.

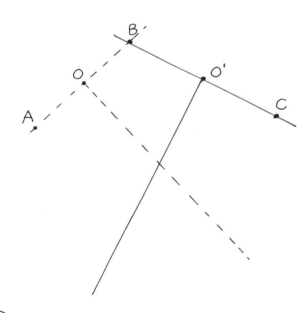

3
Then draw a line between B and C, divide it in half (at O'), and construct another perpendicular line.

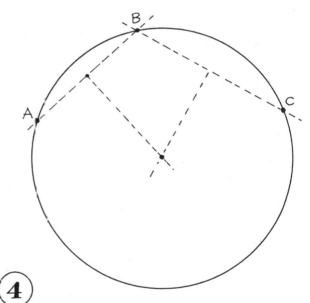

4
Where the perpendicular lines intersect is the center for the circle.

How to cut a paper circle of any size

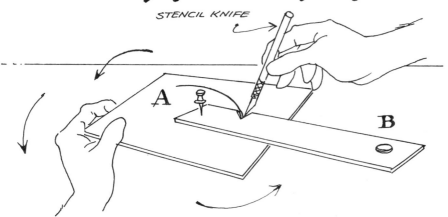

STENCIL KNIFE

A

B

On the paper, A, stick a pushpin firmly through the proposed center of the circle. From this center to the notch cut in the long card is the radius of the circle to be cut. The long strip is a thin card with a pushpin, thumbtack, or other fastener firmly stabilizing the card at B. You cut a circle by rotating the paper around the notch, which holds the stencil knife in position.

How to draw a large circle or arc

A long string or cord can be used for drawing extremely large circles or arcs. Or it may be more convenient for you to use a long strip of cardboard or a long strip of wood. The center of the circle is at A and the strip is secured there. Punch a small hole at the other end, B, to allow for the insertion of a pencil point or the tip of a technical pen that will make the arc line.

At the pen end, B, small blocks of cardboard can be glued near the hole to prevent smudges.

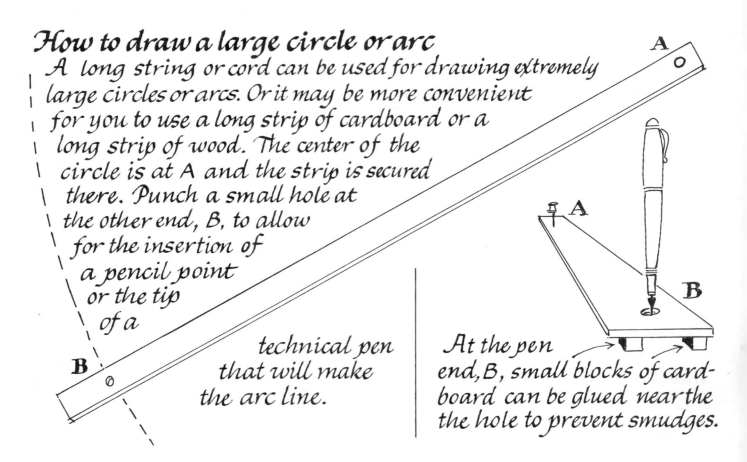

A

B

A

B

How to draw a circle with a brush and compass

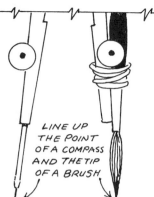

LINE UP THE POINT OF A COMPASS AND THE TIP OF A BRUSH

First remove the lead from the compass and extend the center point out as far as you can to make room for the brush's hair to clear the compass when the brush is attached.

The brush is fastened to the lead leg of the compass with a rubber band, tape, or string. Spread the compass to the desired radius and dip the brush into the ink or paint.

Circles can be drawn freely, quickly, or very carefully this way. Try spread lines and other kinds of lines. Try a dry-brush effect. Experiment with textures of papers. Have fun.

How to sketch a free-hand oval

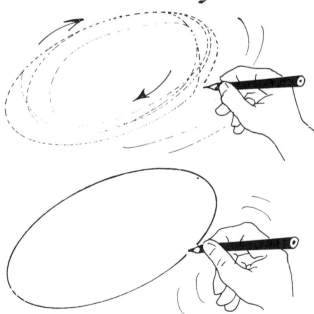

First move your hand and tool in the direction of the oval. The hand and tool move simultaneously.

Take many practice swings, moving the hand and tool quickly, as if you were actually drawing the oval, but not letting your pencil or pen touch the drawing surface.

Finally put the tool to the paper and courageously draw the oval. If you have never done this before, you'll be amazed how well you can sketch ovals, circles, and other forms too.

155

How to draw an oval of any size

Suppose you wish to draw an oval 2⅛" long (major axis) and 1⅝" high (minor axis).

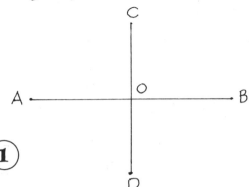

① Draw the major axis AB and the minor axis CD. The axes will be perpendicular to and bisecting each other at O.

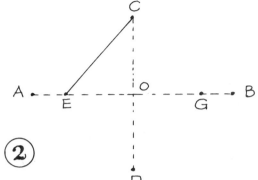

② Find E and G on the major axis. CE and CG are equal to ½ of the major axis (AO or OB).

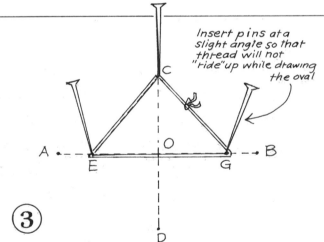

Insert pins at a slight angle so that thread will not "ride" up while drawing the oval

③ Insert pins at 3 points: C, E, and G. Loop a thin strong thread around the bottom of the pins tautly and tie a knot. Then, remove the pin at C.

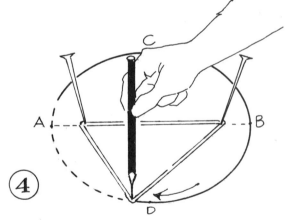

④ When you insert a tool, pencil, or pen into the loop and radiate it around the pins, as shown above, you will draw an oval which passes through points A, B, C, and D.

How to make an oval template

After cutting an oval out of a stiff card sand the edges of the oval with a small piece of sandpaper.

Smooth the curve but...

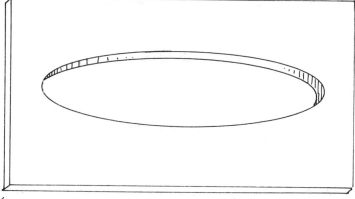

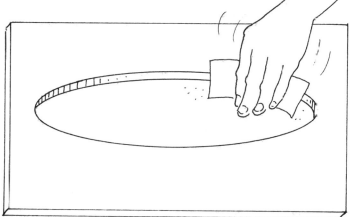

... don't overdo it or you may distort the curve.

Spray front and back with varnish spray to protect the template.

Build up the under-

neath part with small strips of cardboard or tape so that when you use ink, the ink will not blot.

If you use a technical pen, be sure to hold the pen in a vertical position against the edge of the oval.

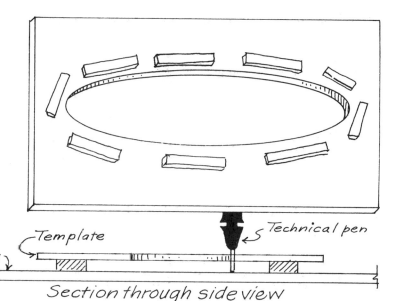

Template   Technical pen

Artwork

Section through side view

How to construct an ellipse by the trammel method

Let AB be the major axis, and CD the minor axis.

They intersect at point O.

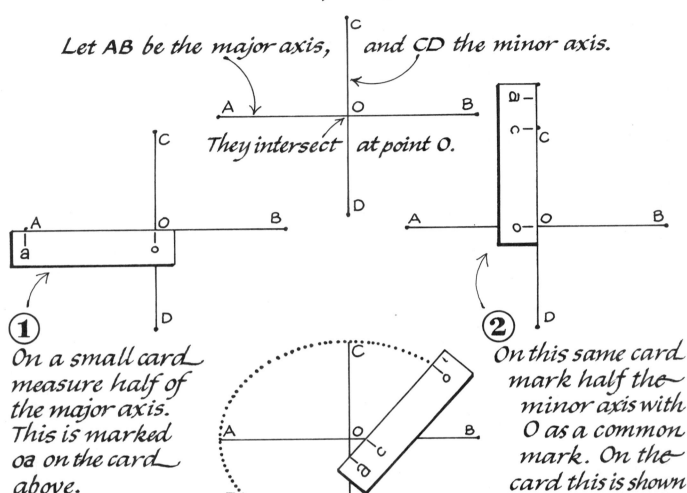

① On a small card measure half of the major axis. This is marked oa on the card above.

② On this same card mark half the minor axis with O as a common mark. On the card this is shown above as oc.

③ You should now have a card that looks like this.

④ On the intersecting axis move this card around to establish all the points on your ellipse. Point a must always be on the <u>minor</u> axis, and the point c must always be on the <u>major</u> axis. Mark the points where o occurs to establish your ellipse.

A machine called an "ellipsograph" is constructed on this same principle.

How to draw an involute (spiral curve)

An involute is a spiral curve. The involute of any polygon may be drawn by extending its sides (as in the two examples below) and, with the corners of the polygon as successive centers, drawing arcs that terminate on the extended sides.

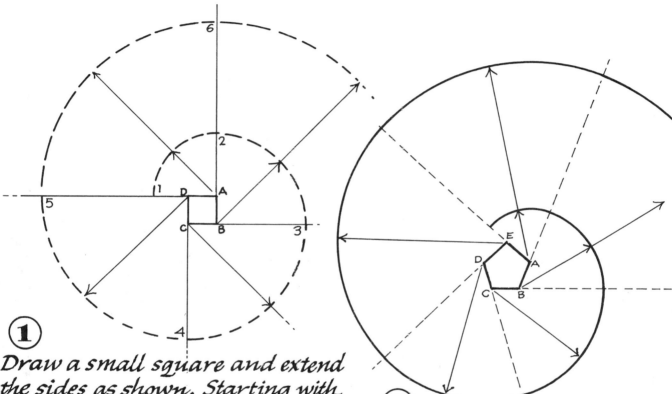

① Draw a small square and extend the sides as shown. Starting with A as a center and A1 as a radius, draw a quarter of a circle, 12. With B as a center and B2 as a radius, draw arc 23. With C as a center and C3 as a radius, draw arc 34. With D as a center and D4 as a radius, draw arc 45. With A as a center and A5 as a radius, draw arc 56 and continue as long as you wish.

② Construct a pentagon ABCDE. Extend the sides as before — these will form the sections where the arcs will meet with A, B, C, D and E as centers, as with the square. Proceed to draw the involute. You can draw involutes with any regular-sided figure.

159

How to draw a spiral with a pencil or pen

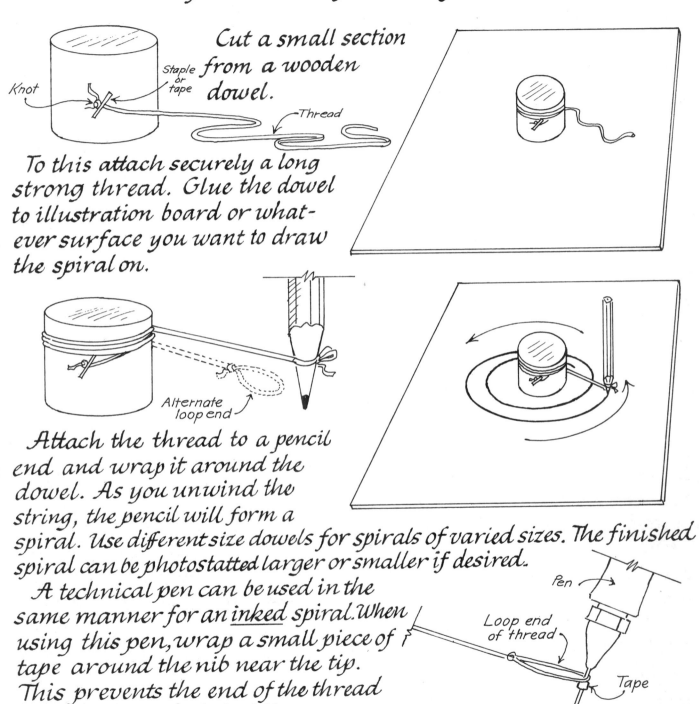

Cut a small section from a wooden dowel.

Knot · Staple or tape · Thread

To this attach securely a long strong thread. Glue the dowel to illustration board or whatever surface you want to draw the spiral on.

Alternate loop end

Attach the thread to a pencil end and wrap it around the dowel. As you unwind the string, the pencil will form a spiral. Use different size dowels for spirals of varied sizes. The finished spiral can be photostatted larger or smaller if desired.

A technical pen can be used in the same manner for an _inked_ spiral. When using this pen, wrap a small piece of tape around the nib near the tip. This prevents the end of the thread from touching the inked line.

Pen · Loop end of thread · Tape

How to "draw" spirals quickly

Slightly curl up the corners of a small card. Attach the card at its center to your drawing board with the aid of a pushpin. Before attaching, rotate the pin around the hole so that the hole is slightly larger than the shank of the push-pin. Hold the brush's tip, with paint, near the card's center. Spin the card with your other hand and immediately apply the brush to the card near the center, and move to the outside as the card spins.

Experiment with different kinds of lines and colors.

How to use a turntable to draw a spiral

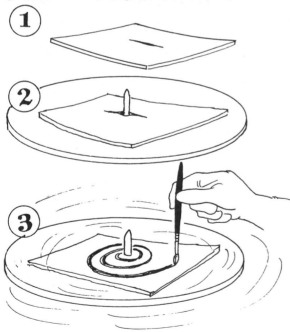

A record player can be used to draw many kinds of free spirals. Take a stiff card and cut a slit as shown in ①. Push the card through the spindle of the turntable ②, ink a brush, turn the player on and have fun ③. Pressure on the brush now and then will create interesting spread line effects.

After drawing one spiral, and while the turntable is still moving, try another color over the one you just completed. Try other effects, like moving the brush to the outside more slowly.

How _any_ regular curve can be made with arcs of circles

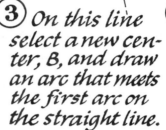

① Draw an arc with the compass. Point A is the center.

② Through this arc draw a straight line.

③ On this line select a new center, B, and draw an arc that meets the first arc on the straight line.

④ Through B draw a straight line, select a new center (C), and draw an arc that meets the last one exactly at one point on the straight line.

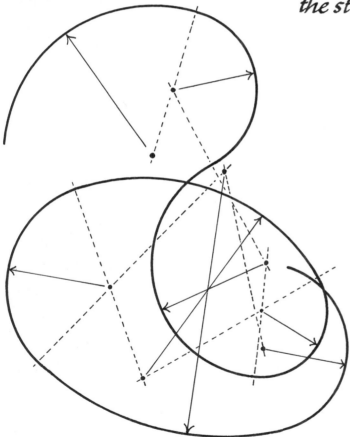

The 4 steps above show the principle by which any regular curved line (one made with arcs of a circle) can be constructed. The essential point is that any 2 consecutive arcs have centers on a common straight line, shown at left with dotted lines ---- the dots are centers of circles used to form the arcs. The consecutive arcs meet at one point only.

The diagram at left is not particularly beautiful. It is drawn for demonstration only.

How to draw a flourished curved line with ellipse templates

In much the same manner as using regular circular arcs to make a curved line ellipse templates can be employed to get a similar curved flourish.

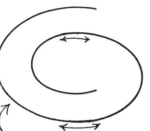

This curve was done with templates. The arrows show the length of overlap common to 2 different sizes.

A variation of the diagram to the left.

Spread line can be filled in.

A spread line can be drawn by moving the template slightly to the left.

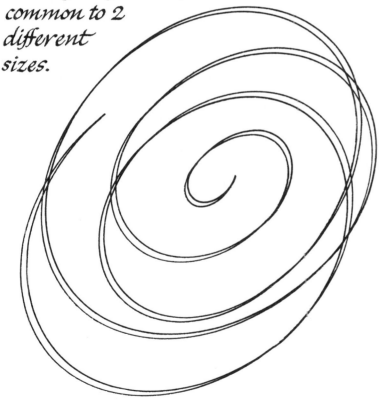

When drawing a curve in this manner, it is good to use only half ellipses. Elliptical joins can be retouched with white paint if necessary.

The flourish to the left is not necessarily beautiful. It was drawn for demonstration purposes only. All arcs and swells were done with templates. Note that these curves do not have the fullness of the flourishes made with arcs of circles.

How to draw repeated irregular images on a curved line

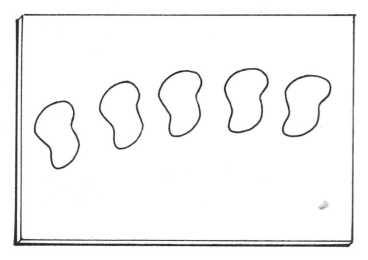

Suppose that you want to draw a design similar to the one at left.

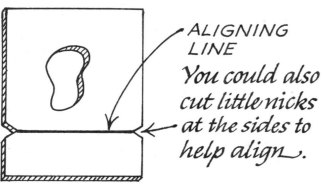

ALIGNING LINE

You could also cut little nicks at the sides to help align.

First cut a template of your image out of cardboard and refine the edges with a gentle rubbing of fine sandpaper. Draw an aligning line under the image.

On your art draw a curved line in pencil as you want it (AB). Your template will align with this line to give you the curve you want for your repeated images. You can build up the template around the edges, gluing little strips of blotting paper or thick cardboard so that your pen will not accidentally smear as you draw the images. Other material (celluloid) can be used to make the template.

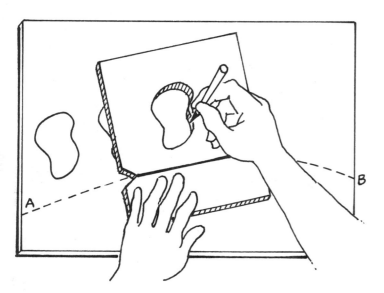

A   B

How to make a template for repeated curves

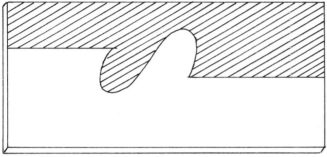

Suppose you want to make a border like this →

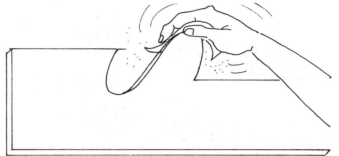

On heavy card with a straight edge bottom, design a curve and cut it out with a mat knife.

Discard the shaded part. Sandpaper the edges to smooth the curve.

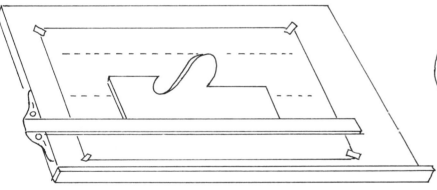

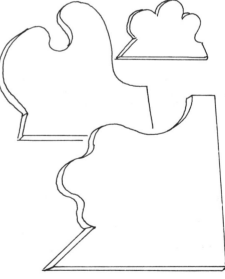

Draw guide lines (see dotted lines above) and space the curves as desired. With a technical pen draw repeats of the curve. Use the template against your Tsquare as you would a regular triangle.

All kinds of variations are possible with this method.

How to draw repeated curved lines in a design

Suppose that you have to draw a curved, or irregular, repeating line as in the example to the left.

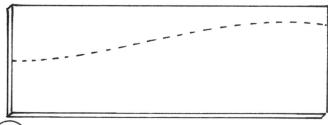

① First design the line on a piece of stiff card or illustration board.

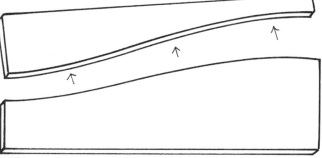

② Then cut this line with a sharp mat knife or stencil knife.

③ Smooth the edge with a piece of fine sandpaper.

④ Lay it on the illustration and repeat it as you designed it. Use a technical pen for inking the line and raise the template with pieces of tape underneath near the inking edge.

How to draw a round corner

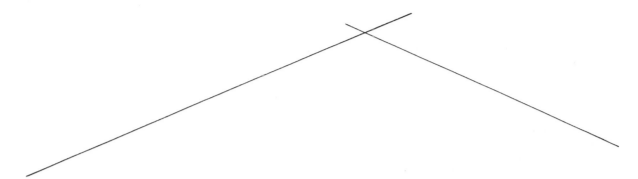

Suppose that you had 2 intersecting lines that form a pointed corner but you want a round corner instead.

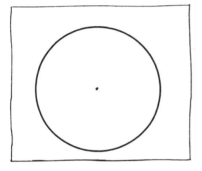

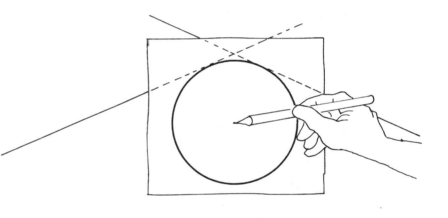

First obtain the curve by drawing a circle of any size you want on a separate piece of paper. An arc of this circle will become the round corner. Move the paper around until the circle is tangent to the 2 intersecting lines. Mark the center of the circle, remove the paper and draw the arc. You now have a round corner.

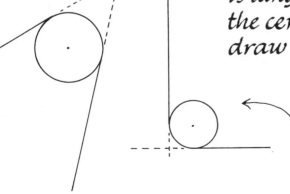

This method can be used for making round corners on any intersecting lines regardless of the angle they make.

How to draw a regular polygon with any number of sides

Assume you want to draw a pentagon and a 5-point star...

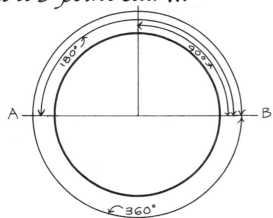

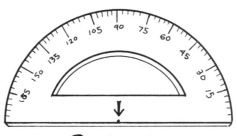

Use a **Protractor** for measuring angles.

On a circle, draw line AB. After dividing 360° (total number of degrees in a circle) by 5 (the desired division) and getting 72°, use the protractor to measure these continuous 72° angles and you will get points A, B, C, D, and E (see below). These points are now joined to form either a pentagon or a 5-pointed star. If you want a six-sided figure, divide 360° by 6 (60°) and proceed as you did with the 5-pointed polygon. If you want a 10-sided figure, divide 360° by 10 (36°), and so on. By trial and error, you must add a little or subtract a little with figures that are not easily divided into 360°.

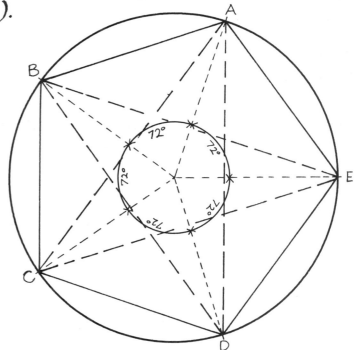

How to draw a *FAT* 5-pointed star

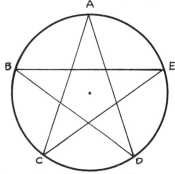

There are 360° in any circle.

A protractor is an instrument for measuring angles. To find 5 equidistant points on the circumference of circle, divide 360° by 5 to get 72°. Using the protractor, you can now get the 5 points on the circle to establish the star.

A 5-pointed star has 5 equidistant points, A, B, C, D, and E, on the circumference of a circle. These points must be established on the circle before you can draw a star.

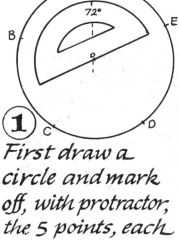

① *First draw a circle and mark off, with protractor, the 5 points, each at a 72° angle from the center.*

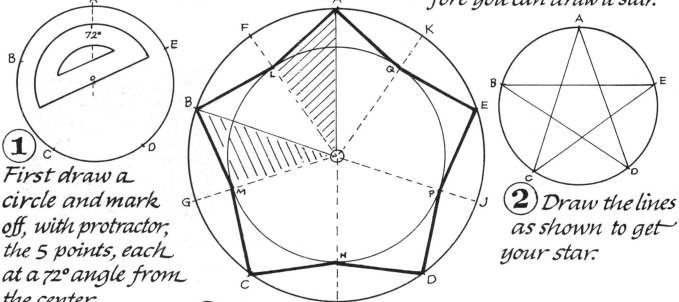

② *Draw the lines as shown to get your star.*

③ *Now find the centers of AB (F), and BC(G), etc., and draw lines from these points through the center of the circle. Draw a circle with any desired radius through these lines, FO, GO, HO, JO, and KO. Draw lines AL, BL, BM, CM, CN, and so on and you will have drawn your 5-pointed star. Shaded effects can be drawn as in section AOG.*

Optical illusions

Illusions in art are fascinating, and most people enjoy them. A few are shown here.

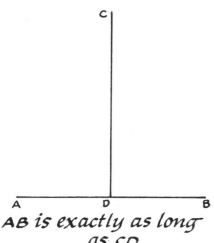

AB *is exactly as long as CD.*

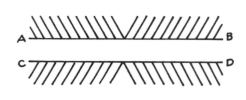

Line AB is parallel to CD.

AB *is parallel to CD.*
LOOK AT IT FROM EXTREME LEFT.

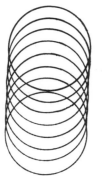

Do you "read" the circles from top to bottom or bottom to top?

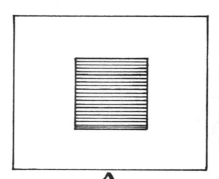

A

B

The gray area in B appears to be lighter than the gray area in A. If the white in A were orange and the gray in A were green, the enclosed square would appear to be blue. If the black in B were blue and the gray in B were green, the square area would appear yellow-green.

AB *appears to be shorter than BC. They are both the same size.*

All boxes to the right are same size.

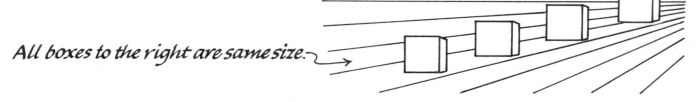

The lopsided figure in the center is a perfect circle.

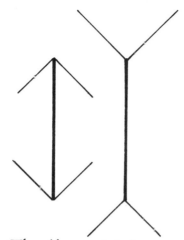

The line at left appears to be smaller than the line to the right. They are both the same length.

The center circle at top appears to be larger than the bottom solid circle. They are both the same.

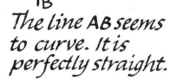

The line AB seems to curve. It is perfectly straight.

The white area to left appears to be much whiter than the white area to the right.

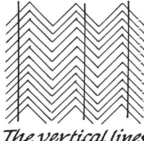

The vertical lines are perfectly parallel.

NOTE

A technique invented in ancient Greece that was popular in France was to paint flat walls with flutes and columns, and very ornate illusions of objects. This style is called "trompe l'oeil."

Painting
How to prepare a porous surface for painting

Blotters, cloth, and other porous materials can be prepared with a spray to minimize bleeding of colors. In the case of T-shirts, for example, stretch the material, spray it with workable or other fixative (varnish), and paint your image. The color may still bleed – but not as much.

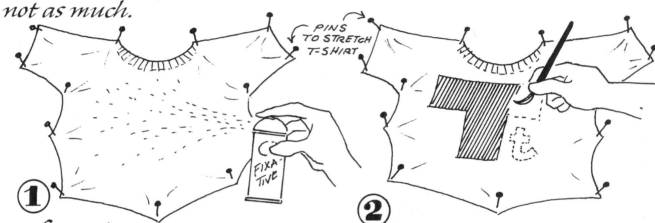

PINS TO STRETCH T-SHIRT

FIXA-TIVE

① Spray in an open area so that you will not breathe the fixative – outdoors, in a closed room with a fan blowing out, in a window, etc.

② Sketch first in pencil and then paint your design. Color used should be waterproof in this instance.

MASK

An interesting effect can be achieved by masking out areas with a blotter or similar porous material, and painting over the entire area. Masked area will have a slightly different value.

How to paint a light-colored object against a dark background when painting a transparent watercolor

Suppose you want to paint a transparent watercolor painting with a light yellow ocher tree against a dark background as in the picture at left. Usually the artist paints around the tree with the dark background color. The method described here is much better because you get sharper definition and can paint over the tree quickly with the background color.

← First sketch out the composition and draw in the tree with a yellow wax crayon.

← Proceed to paint the watercolor until it is finished, except for the tree. When the background color is dry, remove the crayon tree with a wad of cotton and rubber cement thinner. You will find that it can be completely removed, allowing you then to paint in the yellow ocher tree in watercolor.

Foreground grasses, weeds, and light-colored flowers with dark green grass background can also be done in the same manner.

How to use a wash-out technique in making a design

On illustration board paint a design with poster or tempera color.

When the design is dry, paint over the entire area as quickly as you can with waterproof ink.

After the ink has dried, wash the entire board under water. The original design will reappear in bright color and with an interesting quality to the line.

Using this technique with wax crayons and ink on rough mat board will produce a similar effect.

How to clean out an area in a watercolor painting

It is possible to clean out an area for repainting in a watercolor. Follow the instructions below to have another chance on that watercolor done on that expensive paper.

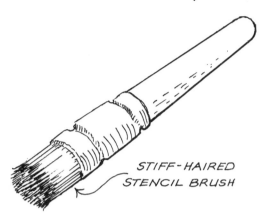

STIFF-HAIRED
STENCIL BRUSH

NOTE! DO NOT SCRUB TOO HARD WITH THE BRUSH — YOU MAY DAMAGE THE FIBERS OF THE PAPER.

Suppose that the dotted-line circled area to the right is not correct and you want to change it. Using a stiff stencil brush and lots of clean water, gently scrub the area, agitating the paint. Use a blotter after a moment to blot up the spot. Have lots of blotting paper handy. Repeat the proceedure, using clean blotting paper each time and lots of clean water, and in time you should have a clean area ready for reworking. For sharp-edged areas use a cutout stencil and brush.

How to paint on shiny and/or glossy surfaces

Any graphic artist knows what a bother it is to paint watercoler or tempera on top of glossy photographs or glossy varnished reproduced art. He invariably has trouble making the paint adhere and <u>stay</u> on the glossy surface. Here are some suggestions that will eliminate this problem.

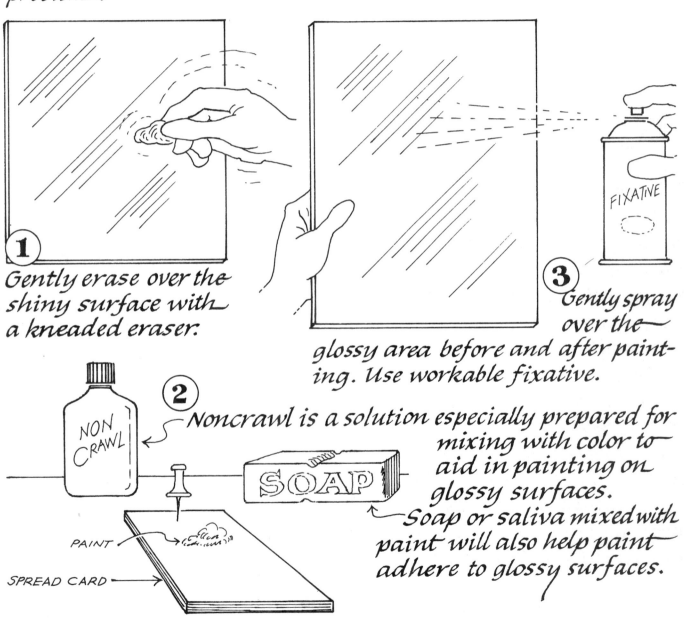

1 Gently erase over the shiny surface with a kneaded eraser.

3 Gently spray over the glossy area before and after painting. Use workable fixative.

2 Noncrawl is a solution especially prepared for mixing with color to aid in painting on glossy surfaces.

NON CRAWL

SOAP

PAINT

SPREAD CARD

Soap or saliva mixed with paint will also help paint adhere to glossy surfaces.

FIXATIVE

How to make watercolor stick to shiny surfaces

Shown here are 3 ways to help water-soluble paint stay on shiny surfaces such as acetate, glass, foil cards, and other shiny surfaces.

If you have trouble keeping water-soluble color adhered, especially for large color areas, mix a little casein glue with tempera, poster color, or other paint and you will find that the paint never comes off.

You must work reasonably fast or the casein may dry up before you are finished with it.

Mucilage can be mixed with the water-soluble paint before using. A small amount of oxgall mixed with the paint is also good.

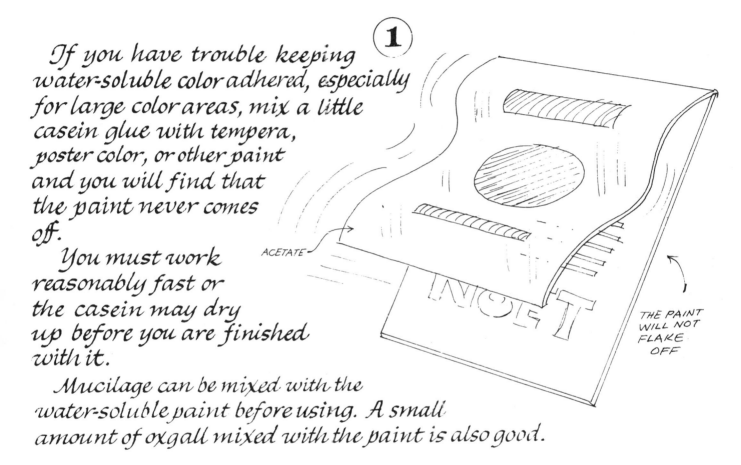

ACETATE

THE PAINT WILL NOT FLAKE OFF

A little soap mixed with the water-soluble paint helps it lay flat and adhere to glossy surfaces. A little saliva has the same effect.

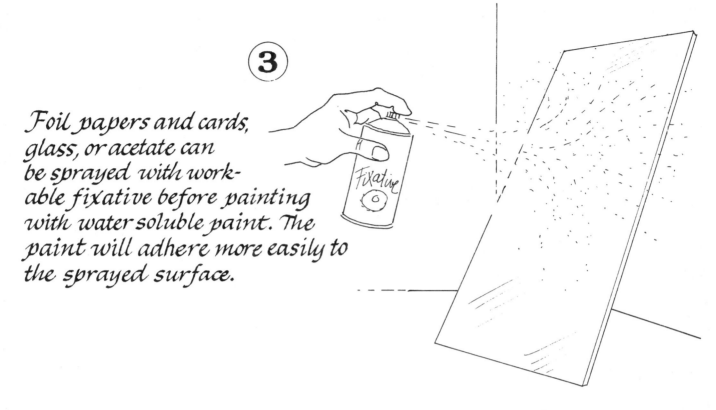

③

Foil papers and cards, glass, or acetate can be sprayed with workable fixative before painting with water soluble paint. The paint will adhere more easily to the sprayed surface.

How to paint with watercolor on a wax surface

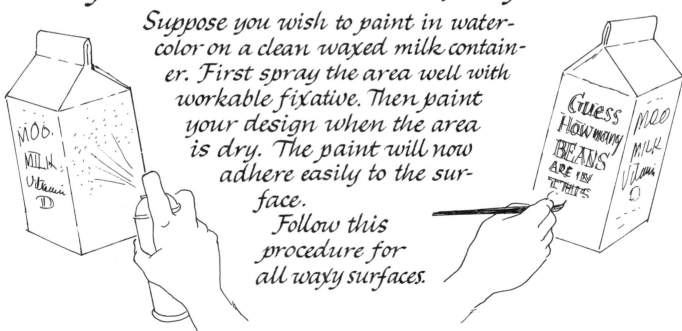

Suppose you wish to paint in watercolor on a clean waxed milk container. First spray the area well with workable fixative. Then paint your design when the area is dry. The paint will now adhere easily to the surface.

Follow this procedure for all waxy surfaces.

How to dry wet art and photos quickly

An invaluable tool in every art and photography studio is a regular hair dryer. It will save so much time that the cost of buying is not prohibitive.

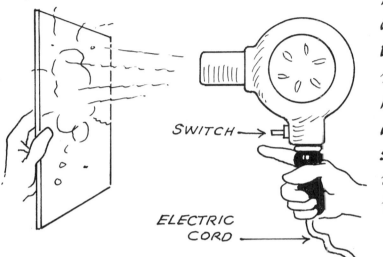

Hold the dryer away from the art or photo. Warm air is blown against the art almost instantaneously. Do not hold too close – you may blur heavily inked lines. Photo prints and photostats can be dried in seconds. Some watercolor artists use the dryer to save precious working time.

SWITCH →

ELECTRIC CORD →

How to make your design more transluscent

You may want your design to be more transluscent – for tracing or photographic purposes. Put your art face down on clean surface and, with a cotton ball or soft rag, spread mineral oil over the back of your sketch. Be sure to clean off all the excess oil with clean rags when you have finished.

MINERAL OIL

BACK OF SKETCH

How to paste a print on a glossy photo

Sometimes when you rubber cement a print to a photograph or photostat — especially a glossy photo — it will not stay adhered.

If you have this trouble...

WHITE TEMPERA

...paint the area to be pasted with white paint.

When the paint is dry, paste the piece on. It should now stay on.

How to draw difficult subjects on acetate or glass

There may be an occasion when it is necessary to draw a complicated subject and you do not have much time. Unusual perspec-
tive views, very complicated pieces of machinery, or a cluttered
scene with unusual architecture are some possible examples of
such subjects. Many times an artist will use a camera in these
situations and later enlarge the picture and use it for reference.
As a substitute you can, however, use a piece of acetate taped to
a heavy mat, hold it steadily at the desired position, and make
a quick sketch with a felt-nib pen. A piece of glass, heavily taped
on the edges for safety, can be used in the same manner. When
you return to the studio, the back of the acetate or glass can be
painted white and, when dry, can be photostatted for a larger
or smaller print — as desired.

As you sketch the subject, your head must remain still. You
can see better, sharper images if you keep one eye closed as
well.

How to use acetate to trace a drawing from a continuous-tone photo

If you want to reduce a continuous-tone photo or picture from a magazine or other source to a piece of line art...

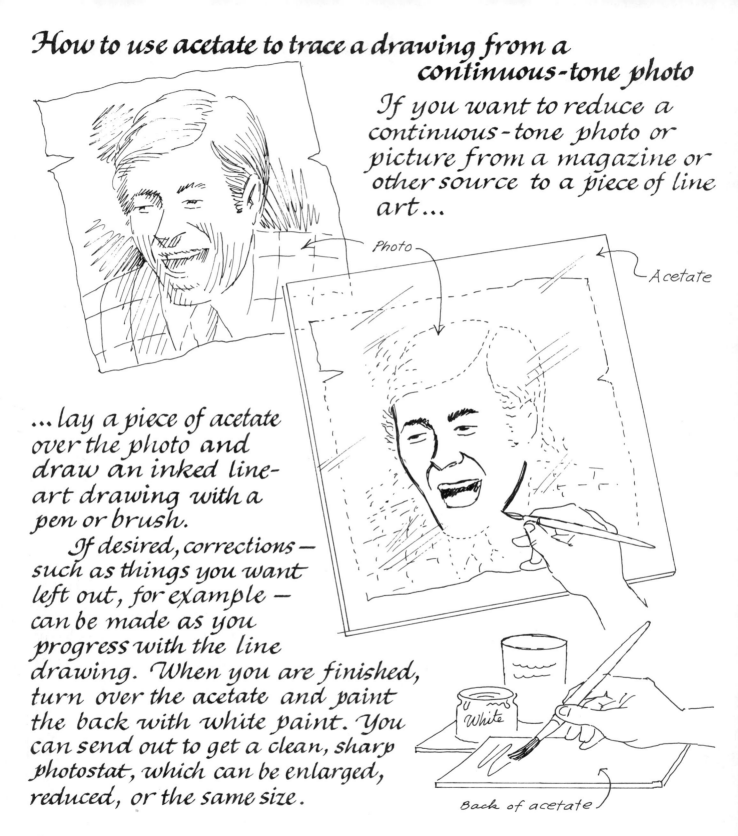

Photo

Acetate

...lay a piece of acetate over the photo and draw an inked line-art drawing with a pen or brush.

If desired, corrections — such as things you want left out, for example — can be made as you progress with the line drawing. When you are finished, turn over the acetate and paint the back with white paint. You can send out to get a clean, sharp photostat, which can be enlarged, reduced, or the same size.

White

Back of acetate

How to draw reverse, or flopped, images

Suppose you have a drawing such as a girl's profile. Instead of facing in one direction you would like it to face the opposite way. Below are a few simple solutions to your problem.

The easiest method is to use a lightbox or home-made equivalent. Simply turn the image over on a lightbox and then trace. A home-made lightbox can be constructed from a plate of glass (frosted is best since it will reduce glare), a light source (fluorescent gives off less heat than incandescent bulbs) and something to prop the glass on. Place the light source under the glass and your turned-over image on top. Trace.

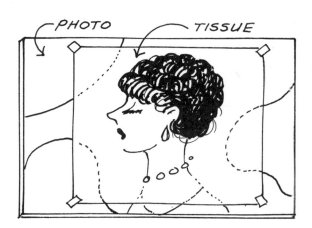

PHOTO   TISSUE

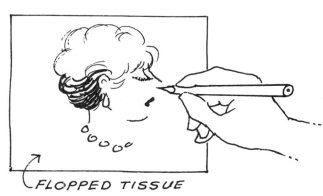

FLOPPED TISSUE

Another method is to trace the art – e.g., a photo – on tissue paper with a good black line (ink, felt nib, soft-pointed pencil). Turn the tissue paper over and redraw (to strengthen) the lines. You can then photostat it larger or smaller. Clear acetate is a great surface for this method.

NOTE.
You can always send your drawing or photo to a commercial photostater and order a "flopped print."

How to soften or modify marker-pen drawings

Turpentine and rubber cement thinner are solvents for most waterproof marker pens. Water is a solvent for the water-soluble markers.

Interesting effects can be obtained by using swabs, Q-tips, rags, and the proper solvent for softening edges and other parts of a drawing already made with marker pens.

Experiment — and see for yourself.

RUBBER CEMENT Thinner

Swabs, Q-tips, cotton balls

TURPS

Turpentine and thinner will clean marker marks and smudges on acetate and most hard nonabsorbent surfaces.

How to get texture effects with spray fixatives

One way to get texture effects, on rocks in a watercolor for example, is to paint the rocks, and, while the paint is still wet, to spray a fixative into the wet areas. Don't overdo it or you will lose the effect. And don't waste any time; work fast. Experiment many times on scrap paper before trying the technique on your art.

Mask

This method can also be used in many cases to get textured effects in the graphic arts as well.

How spray fixative can be used in making a design

There may be an occasion when a subtle value change is required in a design. The design to the left ①is an example. The sky is light red and the hills are the only other image. You want a subtle value change in the sky to suggest a sun. You can do this by cutting a circular stencil, or mask, and using spray fixative. First cut a mask or stencil of a circle for the sun as in ②. Position this mask over your design and spray it with fixative as in ③. The result will be a faint suggestion of a sun in the red sky as in ④.

Dulling spray can be used on shiny metallic surfaces in a similar manner.

When sprayed on coloraid paper a regular spray fixative will give a clouded tint effect.

When workable fixative is sprayed on any surface, you can easily paint with watercolor over the area.

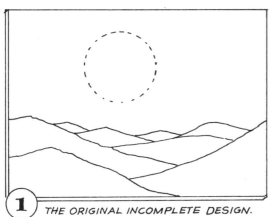

① THE ORIGINAL INCOMPLETE DESIGN. THE DOTTED CIRCLE IS THE SUN'S POSITION FOR SPRAYING WITH FIXATIVE.

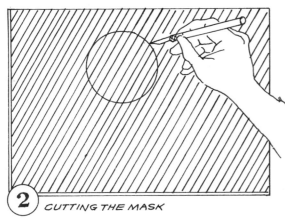

② CUTTING THE MASK

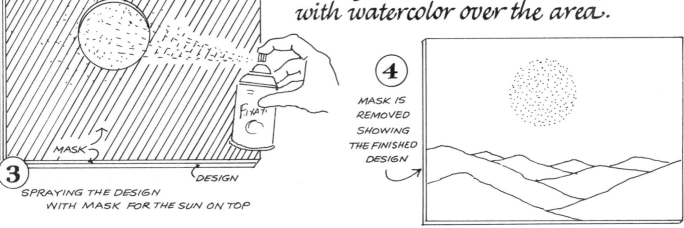

③ SPRAYING THE DESIGN WITH MASK FOR THE SUN ON TOP

MASK

DESIGN

FIXATIF

④ MASK IS REMOVED SHOWING THE FINISHED DESIGN

Easy ways to get straight edges on color blocks and lettering

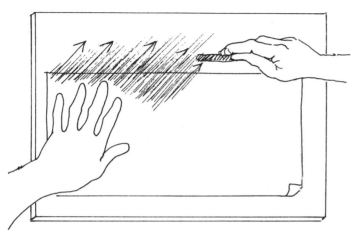

Suppose you wanted to indicate a color area with a straight edge on a layout. Hold a straight-edged paper in the place where you want the straight edge to be. Hold the paper firmly so it does not slip. With a sweeping motion of your ⌐ pencil, pastel, or other tool, and from bottom to top only, swish in strokes across the straight edge, as in the drawing at the left above. When you are finished, remove the paper. You should have an effect similar to the drawing above.

The straight edge of a triangle can be used for drawing straight edges. Hold it firmly where you want the straight edge and bring your tool up to the edge of the triangle, not across the edge.

The straight edge of a piece of paper can be used to align the bottoms of letters in display headlines. When the paper is removed after drawing the letters, the letters will be perfected aligned.

How to get a distorted effect by drawing on white rubber

A piece of white surgical rubber can be purchased in a surgical supply house.

Make Your Salary...
STRETCH

Draw or letter a design on white rubber.

Pull and distort the rubber on a heavy board until you achieve the desired effect. Secure rubber shape well with tape. The board can be sent to the photostatter. The print you get back from him may need retouching because the edges of the images may become fuzzy due to stretching the rubber.

Mechanicals and Paste-ups
How to make a "sandpaper layout"

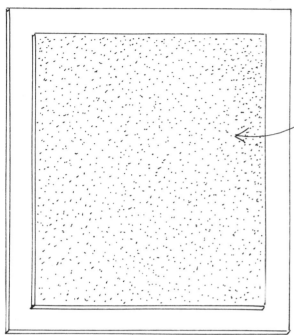

As an aid in developing a layout, you can use the sandpaper technique described here.

First, rubber cement a piece of sandpaper to a piece of illustration board. The size of the sandpaper should be exactly the same as the size of your layout.

On the backs of all your elements (type, logos, illustrations, or anything else), paste small strips of sandpaper.

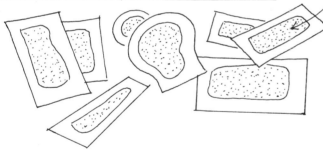

You can then move the pieces around on the large board until you get a satisfactory arrangement.

The sandpaper-backed pieces will adhere readily to the large piece of sandpaper.

Finished layout

Tips on making a mechanical

When drawing a dotted-line box, be sure that corners meet, as in B — never as in A.

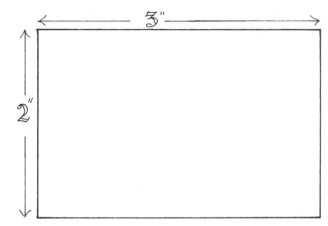

Always give measurements width first, then height. For example, the above rectangle is 3"x 2".

Mechanical paste-up

To be certain that the printer does not make a plate of the photos in paste-ups, draw an "X" in ink through the photostats of tone art being used for positioning on the mechanical.

If a bubble appears on a pasted-down piece, prick the bubble with a push-pin or a knife point and let the air out. Then press down flat around the spot. A strategic slit with a stencil knife may also do the trick. Be careful not to damage the art work, however.

How to dry mount and wet mount with rubber cement
Dry mount

Place the piece to be pasted face down on a clean surface. Spread rubber cement over the back ①. Then spread rubber cement over the area of the mechanical (dotted line) where the piece is to be positioned ②. When both cemented areas are dry, _carefully_ set the rubber-cemented piece in place on the mechanical and apply pressure. A piece of clean tracing paper can be placed under the piece before applying pressure and withdrawn slowly as you dry mount the piece to the mechanical ③.

Wet mount

First, put rubber cement on the area which will receive the piece to be pasted onto the mechanical ①. Next, position the piece, laying it down flat – move it around until it is in the exact position you want ②. Then apply pressure over all. Work relatively fast in the wet method ③. Try to position the piece while the rubber cement is wet. In the dry mount method at top, take all the time you want.

How to paste down wrinkled art work

Suppose that you designed a layout on tracing paper which, for some reason, was discarded. Now that you want to present it, it is a wrinkled mass. Here is what you can do.

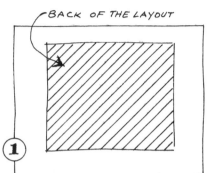

Carefully unravel the layout and coat the back with rubber cement①. Rubber cement the board to which you are going to adhere the layout after marking the position for the top of the layout.②. Over the cemented board, lay 2 pieces of tracing paper that overlap slightly③, just below the mark for the top of the layout.

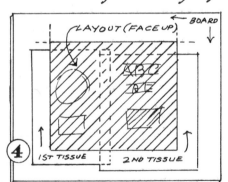

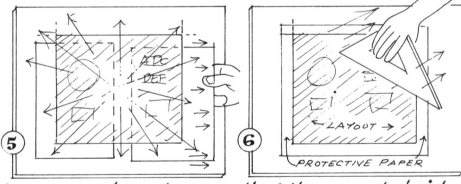

In this overlap area, turn your layout over so that the cemented side is down④. Lay still another piece of tracing paper over the entire area (to protect it) and iron the layout to the board with your hand, always applying pressure from the center out to the edges (arrows)⑤. Now gradually, one at a time, slip the sheets away⑤. Finally, over tracing paper, iron the layout to the board with the edge of a triangle⑥. Clean and trim the layout.

How to paste up a large photostat on a mechanical

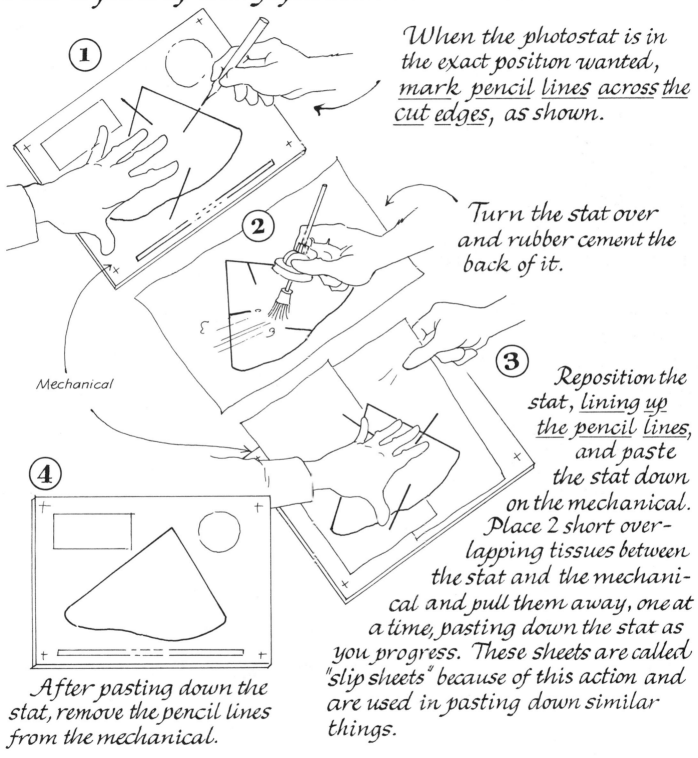

When the photostat is in the exact position wanted, _mark_ _pencil_ _lines_ _across the_ _cut edges_, as shown.

Turn the stat over and rubber cement the back of it.

Reposition the stat, _lining up_ _the pencil lines_, and paste the stat down on the mechanical. Place 2 short overlapping tissues between the stat and the mechanical and pull them away, one at a time, pasting down the stat as you progress. These sheets are called "slip sheets" because of this action and are used in pasting down similar things.

Mechanical

After pasting down the stat, remove the pencil lines from the mechanical.

193

How to avoid cut marks on stats when making a negative paste-up

Tissue layout

The negative paste-up. All negative black photostats have been pasted in position onto a black cardboard.

Negative stat

Tweezers

If you paste up many negative photostats or prints onto a black background (whether it is card, paper, or any other material), you should paint the edges black on every negative print before pasting it down. Otherwise the cut edges, being white on the negative paste-up, will be black marks on the positive print that you get back from the photostatter.

Waterproof black ink should be applied to the white edges of all the negative photostats with a brush, as shown, before pasting them in position on the black card.

First paste rubber cement on the backs of all stats. Next, trim them close to the images, and then paint with black ink. Apply rubber cement over the entire area of the black card. Flap a tissue layout over this card so that you can position the stats exactly where you want them when you paste them down.

How to be sure your mechanical paste-up has no excess cement

If you have
been missing
too many rubber
cement spots on your
mechanicals that should
have been cleaned off, hold
your paste-up to a light and you
will be able to see easily any excess
rubber cement you missed in cleaning
up. You can also hold the mechanical to the window light; just move it
around and you will see the neglected spots.

How to use an old telephone book as an aid in paste-up

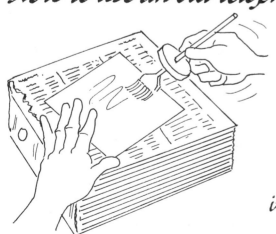

An old telephone book, or a similar catalogue,
is great as a back up for brushing rubber
cement on things to be pasted up on mechanicals or other surfaces. After using the top
page, it can be discarded, and then the
next clean page is ready for use.

A pile of newspaper pages is also a handy
item to have around for a similar purpose.

How to clean wax from a mechanical

Suppose that you use a waxer instead of rubber cement to adhere elements on to a mechanical and you want to reposition something that is already adhered. You want to file away the piece you remove but you do not want it to stick to other pieces in your file cabinet. The demonstration below should help you solve this problem.

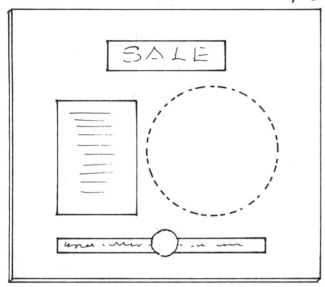

MECHANICAL
The dotted area above is wax left after item has been removed. You now want to clean the area.

With the back end of a metal ruler or the end edge of a small, stiff piece of cardboard scrape the wax off the mechanical. Then clean the area with a wad of cotton and rubber-cement thinner.

Excess wax can be cleaned from the edge of the ruler with your thumbnail.

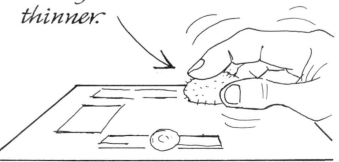

How to show crop marks on a photo and other art

Crop marks show the part of a picture that you want the printer to make a plate for. When you show the marks, you want to save the rest of the art for possible future use. <u>Never</u> draw crop marks right on the art. Show them as in the examples below.

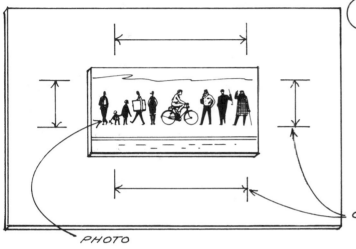

PHOTO

CROP MARKS

① First mount your photo or art (if it does not already have a wide mat of white). In this margin show the area that you want to be printed. The board that it is mounted on will also reinforce the art.

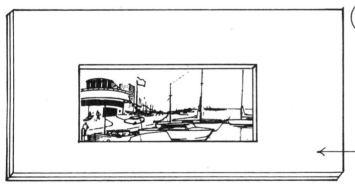

MAT

② Another method is to cut a mat of the area that you want. This may be an odd mat, but it is not for framing.

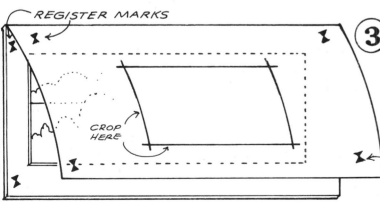

REGISTER MARKS

CROP HERE

③ Another method is to show the picture area on a vellum flap (don't forget to include register marks for greater accuracy).

NORMALLY THE REGISTER MARKS ARE CLOSER TO THE CROP AREA THAN SHOWN HERE.

197

How to "eliminate" cut marks on a mechanical

When you are working on a paste-up, mechanical, or any design in which many images are pasted down, it is sometimes difficult to evaluate the design because the shadows of the cut marks around the elements show and it is hard to appraise the relationships.

To minimize these cut marks, making it easier to evaluate your design, hold your paste-up towards a light source so that you are looking at your design in shadow.

How to make an acetate overlay on a mechanical

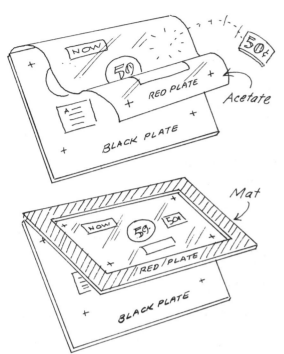

Sometimes you may have a flexible acetate overlay on a mechanical upon which you paste other items which then sometimes flip off as the mechanical is moved around.

To prevent, or minimize, the possibility of these items flipping off, prepare a stiff board mat (made of card) for the acetate. This mat will hinge rigidly on the mechanical and not bend so that items pasted down will have a better chance of staying on.

How to make a color overlay on a mechanical

If you have a mechanical paste-up with many elements cemented thereon which are thick and heavy or of varying weights, the job of making a tissue overlay for color break, or other reasons, will be much simpler if, before any indications are made on the overlay, you insert a piece of heavy acetate between the mechanical and the tissue.

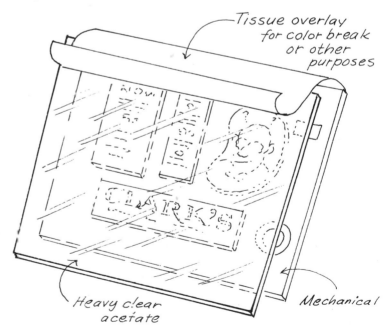

How to prepare a photograph for the printer

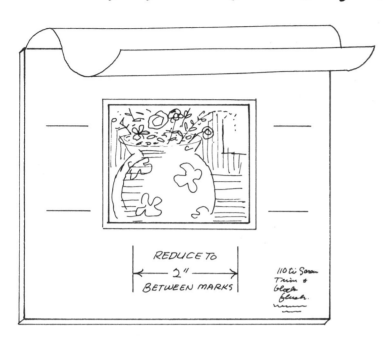

REDUCE TO
2"
BETWEEN MARKS

110 bi Screen
Trim &
bleed
flush.

Always carefully dry mount photographs on heavy card or illustration board, leaving wide borders, as shown. The card must have a flap that acts as a protective covering.

Specifications to the printer are written on the card's borders or on a tissue flap over the photograph—*never* directly on the photograph. If you give instructions on the tissue overlay, be sure the photo's surface is protected by a piece of heavy acetate before you start writing.

If you have a retouched photograph or expensive or delicate art, make a heavy mat, thick enough to protect the face of the art. A *heavy* cardboard flap should be taped to the top and hinge over the art.

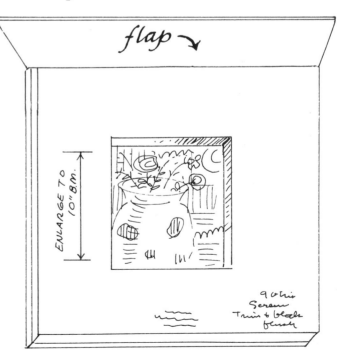

flap

ENLARGE TO 10" 8.m.

9 bi
Screen
Trim & bleed
flush

Photographs, Photostats and Photocopies
How to work with photographs

Never write instructions on the back of a photograph – especially not with a hard ball-point pen …

… or a marker pen. The ink of a marker pen may bleed through and stain the photo on the other side.

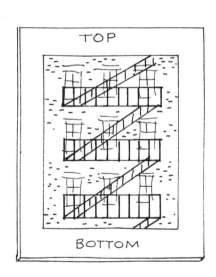

A stabilo pencil is made especially for writing on glossy surfaces.

Always mark TOP and BOTTOM on all photos, particularly on photos in which the subject is not easily recognized.

Always ask for margins on photos where you can mark instructions.

How to retouch a photograph with laundry bleach

Photo, before retouching

Swabbing bleach on the area to be removed.

Household bleach can be used on photographs and photostats (line or continuous tone art) to bleach out unwanted areas or lines and return the retouched area to absolute white of the print. Use a Q-tip or a cotton ball as a swab. Apply the bleach by gently rubbing the image to be eliminated. Blotters should be kept handy to help dry the wet area.

Always protect eyes and mouth from bleach. Cap bleach container when not in use. The Silver Genie pens achieve the same result. The bleaching pen, fine or broad felt tip, is used to retouch the photostat. It leaves a yellow stain where it has erased the image. Mark over these spots with the fixing pen. Finally, rinse your photostat under cool water and air dry (or use a hand-held hair-gun).

How to make a 3-D design photographically

If you want a repeated element in a design, such as the one to the right, you can accomplish this in a simple photographic way by first lettering the elementary design horizontally

When the lettering is finished, attach it, as shown, to a large cardboard tube or cylinder. Give the photographer or photostatter a focal point where he is to center his lens. If you want the design to curve down, the focal point on the cylinder is above the design as in ①. If you want it to curve up, the focal point is below as in ②.

A strip of 5 vertical designs can be photographed 2 times, for example, and finally assembled in the form shown at the top.

The design can be attached on the tube in different positions from the one shown. Try some of your own.

How to order photostats

A photostat is an inexpensive photographic image usually done on cheap photostat paper. <u>Glossy</u> photostats are normally ordered for line art and <u>mat</u> for continuous tone art. If you have your own photostat-machine, you can set your own system for ordering them. Prints are made in a single step and referred to as direct positives (DP or PMT). To achieve a white-on-black image ask for either a reverse or a paper negative (distinguished from a film negative which is clear in the non-black areas). For an image reversed directionally from left to right order a flop (not a reverse). Photostats can also be made on acetate. Photostats for direct to plate printing should be RREU (right-reading, emulsion up). RREU acetates are used for digital pre-press, photosilkscreening and polymer plate imaging.

Do not use marker pens for writing instructions on a photostat. They may bleed through and spoil the print.

Sizing photostats can be done with a calculator or a proportion wheel. The calculator is more accurate, but the stat camera can only be focused in .5% increments. The proportion wheel lets you see several related proportions at once, such as height and width.

Always write your name and company on every photostat

A sample instruction looks like this →

1 Glossy print at 54%
Jonathan Thompson
Beejay Company

How to "gang-up" photostats and save money

When ordering photostats, use up all the space that you are paying for in the print you will get back. Check the sizes and prices of prints with your photostatter.

Put as many images on your original copy as you can within the limits of the stat size you will get back. This method of putting more than 1 image on your original is called "ganging-up".

Original marked-up Copy

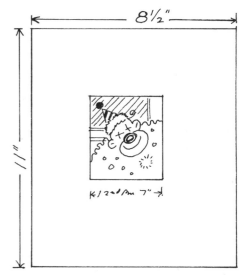

Photostat, as ordered. Wasted space could have been used for other stat material.

Original marked-up copy correctly filled

Photostat of your original, with no wasted space

Fill up all of the space you are paying for with all kind of useable items (such as logos, for example) in addition to the illustrations.

How to position art in your own photostat machine

If you have a photostat machine in your studio and have been wasting prints because you are not positioning your art on the copyboard correctly in relation to the negative before printing keep 2 large L-shaped pieces of black cards handy and use as shown below. You should have no trouble henceforth by wasting prints — and money.

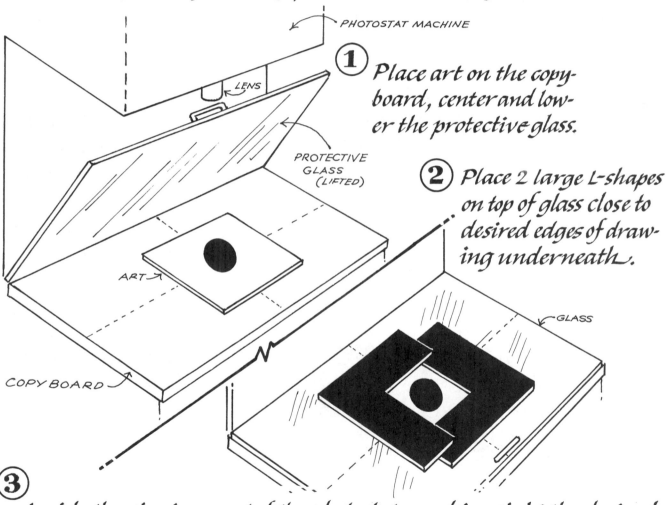

PHOTOSTAT MACHINE

LENS

① Place art on the copyboard, center and lower the protective glass.

PROTECTIVE GLASS (LIFTED)

② Place 2 large L-shapes on top of glass close to desired edges of drawing underneath.

ART

GLASS

COPY BOARD

③ Inside the viewing part of the photostat machine sight the desired area, which is easier to see because of the black edges. Position your negative accordingly and shoot. No more wasted prints!!

How to get good copier prints of tracing paper designs

Most of the models of copying or duplicating machines have buttons to push if you want darker prints. If you use tracing paper (or other trans-luscent-paper) drawings or designs, you must back up with white card or heavy opaque paper to get a good print – even though the button on the machine is pushed for more contrast. Black ink drawings on frosted acetate are handled in the same way.

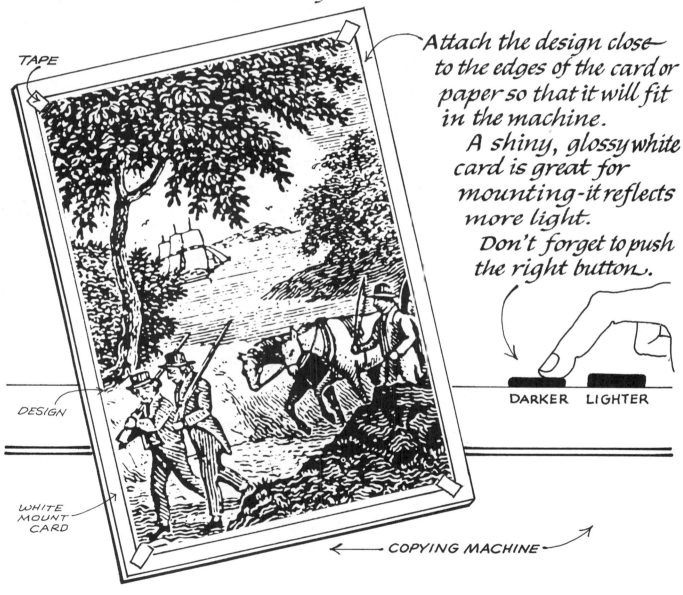

TAPE

DESIGN

WHITE
MOUNT
CARD

Attach the design close to the edges of the card or paper so that it will fit in the machine.

A shiny, glossy white card is great for mounting-it reflects more light.

Don't forget to push the right button.

DARKER   LIGHTER

← COPYING MACHINE →

Photocopiers, many of them digital, can do nearly anything that a photostat camera can. Photocopying can be done onto many different paper stocks, including tracing paper and acetate. Try a test sheet before using a rough surface paper. The irregular surface make break up your image. Use an old iron to heat and smooth the surface. Copier machines also have trouble with thick sheets.

Photocopy machines can enlarge or reduce your image. Most machines are limited to a range between 64% and 141%. Some allow 1% increments while others have fixed focuses. Digital copiers usually range from 50% to 400%. When reducing or enlarging images beyond the available limits use two or more steps. Beware of degradation of the image. Calculate your steps in advance. For example, to reduce 50% in two steps use 67% and 75%; to reach 40% add a third step of 80%; to reach 33% add a third step of 67%; etc.

Digital color copiers can also manipulate the image (rotate, flop and skew), crop it or do bitmapped editing.

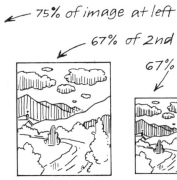

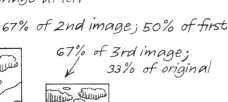

75% of image at left

67% of 2nd image; 50% of first

67% of 3rd image; 33% of original

Printing:
The four major processes of printing

The four processes of printing are shown below. The difference in the plates is the major difference in the process, although there are many others that are important — the construction of the machines, the kinds of paper and ink best for each, etc.

LETTERPRESS
(RELIEF PROCESS)

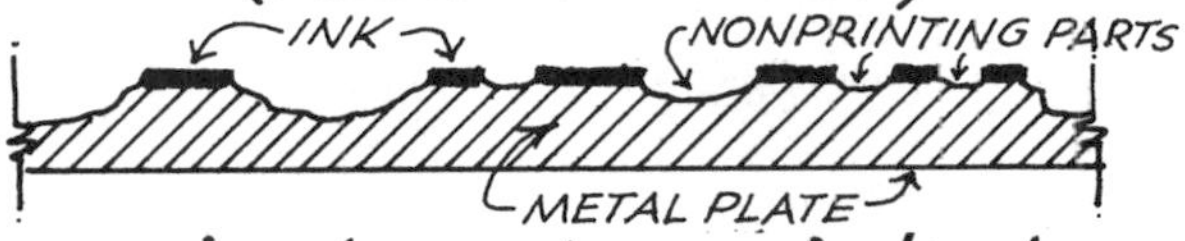

The raised parts are inked and impressed into the paper to create the image. Plates are made from zinc, magnesium or polymer. Metal plates are mounted on type-high blocks of wood. Polymer plates require a special type-high magnetic base.

LITHOGRAPHY
(PLANOGRAPHIC PROCESS)

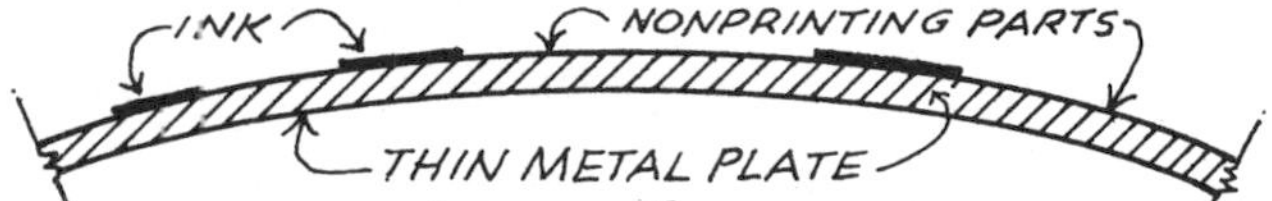

Lithography (offset in commercial printing) prints images by dampening the surface of the plate (the nonprinting parts) with moisture and preparing the image area to receive the greasy ink. Printing is possible because grease rejects water.

GRAVURE
(INTAGLIO PROCESS)

Gravure (usually rotogravure, because the plate is a large circular cylinder) is the opposite of letterpress. The plate is inked and the nonprinting raised parts of the plate are wiped clean by a "doctor blade."

SILKSCREEN
(STENCIL PROCESS)

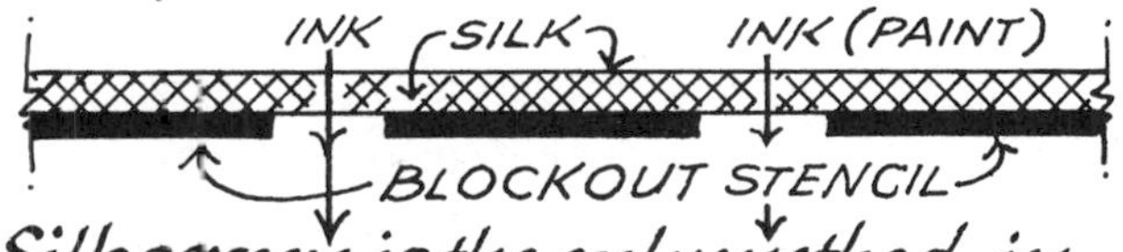

Silkscreen is the only method in which, with the use of a rubber squeegee, the paint, or ink, is squeezed through the plate. The blockout is the stencil adhered to the silk. It is hand-cut or composed photographically.

209

Other processes or methods of printing

There are other printing processes, but they are used mostly for small runs. The one exception is Flexography, which is extremely fast.

Flexography is a letterpress method in which fast-drying inks are used on speed presses. The process is designed for printing on cellophane (bags, covers, etc.). It is a major process in terms of volume of work. It prints from rubber plates.

Collotype is a gelatin process in which the plate "absorbs" the image so that it can be inked and impressed onto paper. Tone areas in the art are not screened, as in other processes, and the printed images are continuous in tone. This technique is used almost exclusively for picture postcards. It is one of the few processes that prints continuous-tone impressions.

Mimeograph is an office machine that prints by a stencil method similar to silk screen. Images can be drawn on the stencil.

Direct Lithography images are drawn in reverse on a large stone with a greasy solution. The nonprinting parts are moistened with water. The resulting lithographs (Daumier, Munch, etc.) tend to be in the fine-arts area and are seldom used in commercial printing, except to furnish a print for further reproduction by one of the major processes. Lithographs have a grainy look.

Etchings and Woodcuts are fine-arts processes. Etchings are intaglio prints while woodcuts are relief prints. Engraving (copper or steel) is another intaglio process.

Photographs and Photostats are photographic processes. Cibachromes and C-prints are high-quality photographs often used for small runs of images in place of color lithography.

Thermography is raised printing that is heat-induced. The printed images look like engraving.

Photocopying is a photographic powder transfer method of reproducing an image. Full color digital photocopiers can edit and manipulate images like a computer.

Ozalids and Diazos (blueprints and brownprints) are chemical processes that produce a bluish or brownish toned image using specially treated papers. Associated with architects and engineers they can also be useful to the designer because of their cheapness and wide range of available sizes.

Laser and inkjet printers are used with computers. The laser printer is similar to a photocopier. The inkjet printer prints by squirting thin streams of ink at the paper.

How to make your own rubber stamp

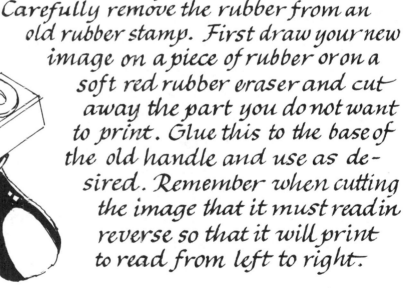

Carefully remove the rubber from an old rubber stamp. First draw your new image on a piece of rubber or on a soft red rubber eraser and cut away the part you do not want to print. Glue this to the base of the old handle and use as desired. Remember when cutting the image that it must read in reverse so that it will print to read from left to right.

Different kinds of printing papers

In order of increasing smoothness, the finishes of paper are: antique, eggshell, vellum, machine finish (MF), and English finish (EF). Additional smoothness is obtained by super calendering (SC). Some finishes, such as linen, tweed, pebble, and cloud, are embossed as the paper leaves the machine. Characteristics of printing paper for the designer to consider are the grain (fiber direction) for folding, basic weight, strength, print quality, color, brightness, opacity, gloss, and refractiveness.

Kinds of printing papers, their uses and sizes

<u>Bond</u> paper is commonly used for letters. It accepts ink readily, is easily erased, and usually comes in 8½" x 11" size sheets.

<u>Coated</u> paper refers to a regular paper that has been given a smooth, glossy coating. It is used when high printing quality is desired. (25"x38")

<u>Text</u> papers come in interesting textures and colors. They are used for special announcements, booklets, and brochures. (25" x 38")

<u>Cover</u> papers are coated text papers in heavier weights and matching colors. They are used for booklet covers primarily. (20"x 26")

<u>Book</u> paper is used for trade and text books and comes with antique or smooth finish. It is less expensive than text papers. (25"x38")

<u>Offset</u> paper is similar to coated and uncoated book paper. It is made primarily for offset lithography printing. (25" x 38")

<u>Index</u> paper is stiff and receives writing ink easily. It comes in smooth and antique finishes and is inexpensive. (22½" x 35" and 25½"x30½")

<u>Newsprint</u> paper, used for newspapers, is also inexpensive. It is very absorbent. (24"x 36)

<u>Tag</u> paper is tinted on one or both sides. It has good bend quality and with a surface good for practically all purposes. (24"x 36)

If you have a question about paper, ask your production department or call your local paper dealer.

European (metric) paper sizes

Europeans and the British use different paper sizes from those prevalent in the United States. While our sizes are seemingly arbitrary theirs are rationally graded, based on multiples of Golden Section sizes. Each size is ½ as big as the preceding one. They are called the A series:

A0 841 × 1189 mm   A1 594 × 841 mm   A2 420 × 594 mm
A3 297 × 420 mm   A4 210 × 297 mm   A5 148 × 210 mm
A6 105 × 148 mm   A7 74 × 105 mm   A8 52 × 74 mm
A9 37 × 52 mm   A10 26 × 37 mm

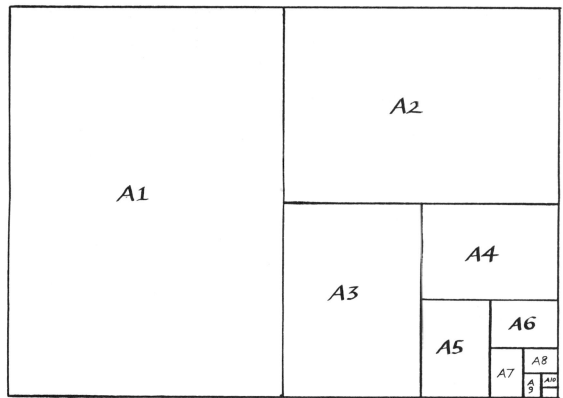

A0 sheet of paper (reduced)

There is also a B series of paper sizes that range from B0 1000 × 1414 mm to B10 31 × 44 mm. Each size is ½ as big as the preceding one.

How to make your own silkscreen set-up

Silkscreen (screen process) is a stencil method of printing posters, prints, wallpaper, T-shirts – just about anything. Below are the parts, and on the next page is the technique.

The FRAME

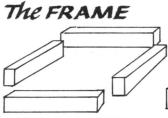

4 PIECES OF WOOD, 2 EACH OF 2 LENGTHS, 2" X 3" IN THICKNESS, ARE ATTACHED AT CORNERS.

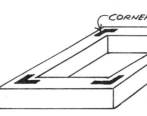

CORNER BRACES

THE CORNERS CAN BE BRACED WITH FLAT METAL ANGLES.

A PIECE OF SILK IS ATTACHED TO FRAME, WHICH IS TURNED OVER, ANGLE SIDE DOWN.

SILK CAN BE STAPLED OR TACKED IN THE SEQUENCE SHOWN ABOVE. ARROWS SHOW DIRECTION OF PULL AS YOU ATTACH.

The STENCIL

WITH TUSCHE INK YOUR DESIGN CAN BE PAINTED RIGHT ON STRETCHED SILK. GLUE, THEN SPREAD ALL OVER, AND, WHEN DRY, REMOVE TUSCHE WITH WASH OF KEROSENE.

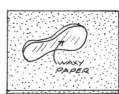

BROWN KRAFT PAPER CAN BE CUT AND ATTACHED TO SCREEN WHEN STENCIL IS CUT.

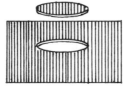

WAXY PAPER

AMBER LACQUER FILM (2 PLY) CAN BE CUT AND ADHERED WITH LACQUER THINNER.

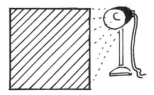

STENCILS CAN BE MADE PHOTOGRAPHICALLY.

The PAINT

WATER COLOR

WATERCOLOR CAN BE USED IF THE STENCIL IS WATER-REPELLENT, AS IN THE LACQUER-BASED FILM.

Silk Screen PAINT

RED ORANGE

CANS OF SPECIAL FINE-GROUND SCREEN PAINT CAN BE BOUGHT. THEY ARE OIL-BASED.

LACQUER

ENAMEL

LACQUER AND ENAMEL PAINTS ARE USED FOR WOOD, METAL, GLASS, ETC.

ACCESSORIES

RUBBER SQUEEGEE, TURPENTINE AND KEROSENE THINNERS, LIQUID GLUE FOR BLOCKOUT, TAPE FOR SEALING CORNERS, SMALL CARDS FOR REGISTERING, PAPER AND CARDS TO PRINT ON.

Be careful with kerosene thinners and lacquer paints. Wear a protective respirator at all times (not a paper mask) and keep your working area well-ventilated.

Silkscreen printing

After the frame is built, the silk stretched, the stencil made and adhered to the screen, the paint mixed, and the paper stacked conveniently for printing you are ready to print.

CLOTHESLINE FOR HANGING PRINTS TO DRY

STRONG SPRING

PAPER OR CARDS

HINGES

HINGE CLAMP

The screen (plate) is lowered and held down. Paint (buttery texture) is added to one end of the screen. The squeegee carries the paint across the stencil and prints onto the paper, which you have positioned against the register marks on the baseboard before lowering the screen. After printing the print is hung on the clothesline to dry. Put the next sheet of paper on the baseboard against the register marks, lower the screen, and squeegee the paint across the stencil, this time in the reverse direction. Continue the operation until all the papers are printed. Clean the screen with proper paint thinner and tools (squeegee), and you are ready for your next job.

The post setup shown at top is fine, but you need only a strip of wood on the edge of the frame to hold the screen up. It can be kicked to lower the screen with your left hand.

FRAME →

SCREW WITH LARGE HOLE IN STICK

HINGE CLAMP

BASE

SIDE VIEW

215

How to print blended color by silkscreen

Beautiful blended-color effects are possible with silkscreen, as described below.

With the screen in a slightly elevated position, deposit small amounts of pastelike color (not too thin) side by side at the inside-hinge end of the screen. Plan your color sequence and have all your colors mixed before depositing them on the screen. They can be deposited with tongue depressors, one for each color, which can be thrown away later. If paint is to come to edge of paper (cropped when dry), you must allow for this extra paper - which is larger than trim will be. With paper or card in position on baseboard, move squeegee back and forth across your screen in an oscillating motion and print your color. The first prints may be streaky, but streaks will eventually disappear.

Do not turn squeegee around as you continue printing. Work fast and you should get 20+ prints before cleaning and doing more. Cleaned-off paint can be saved, mixed, and used again as a neutral color on another job.

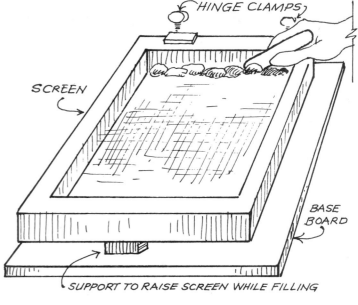

HINGE CLAMPS

SCREEN

BASE BOARD

SUPPORT TO RAISE SCREEN WHILE FILLING

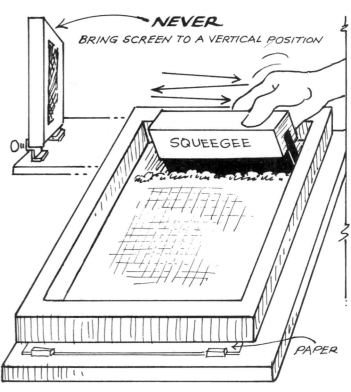

NEVER
BRING SCREEN TO A VERTICAL POSITION

SQUEEGEE

PAPER

Forms of printed matter

Most all printed matter can be classified under one of the divisions below. All artists dealing with printing should know the correct names of these forms. You may be asked to design one.

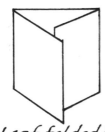

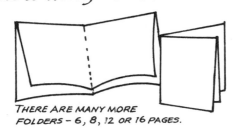

Leaf printed on one side and folded to form 4 pages is a _french fold_.

THERE ARE MANY MORE FOLDERS – 6, 8, 12 OR 16 PAGES.

Single leaf is a _leaf_ or _sheet_.

Leaf folded into two or more folds is a _folder_.

In the case of booklets or book forms the sheets, once folded, are gathered together in order, and the _signatures_ (folded sheets) are _collated_. After all the signatures are collated, they are stitched together by either of the two methods shown below.

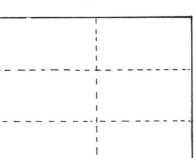

Large leaf folded to make a large, finished folder is a _broadside_.

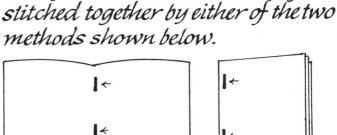

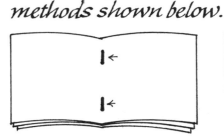

SADDLE STITCH
STAPLES (ARROWS) ARE FORCED THROUGH THE BACKBONE IN THE EXACT CENTER OF THE FOLDED SIGNATURES

SIDE STITCH
STAPLES ARE FORCED IN SIDE 1/8"– 1/4" FROM BIND SIDE. BOOK CAN-NOT LIE FLAT WHILE OPENED. COVERS ARE GLUED ON.

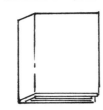

Book form with paper cover is _booklet_ or _pamphlet_. If exquisitely designed it is a _brochure_.

Book form sewn and bound is a _book_. If cover is paper, it is called a _paperback_.

Booklets have a final finishing operation called _trimming_. The top and bottom and one side are trimmed with a guillotine paper cutter. In large editions 3 knives are used to trim all 3 sides at once.

217

Forms of binding

Books and booklets are bound together by one of the processes shown below (if not bound by side-wire or saddle-wire stitching).

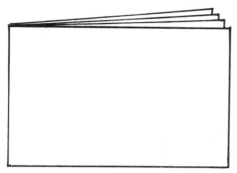

Adhesive binding, ALSO KNOWN AS PERFECT BINDING. PAGES LIE FLAT WHEN OPEN. IT IS NOT A DURABLE BINDING.

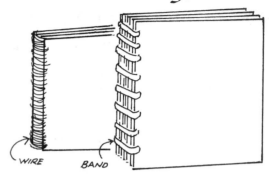

WIRE   BAND

Spiral or mechanical binding. PAGES ARE PUNCHED SO THAT METAL OR PLASTIC WIRES OR BANDS CAN BE WOVEN THROUGH.

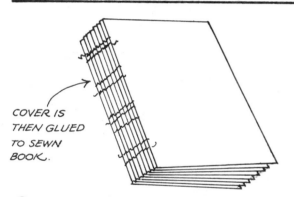

COVER IS THEN GLUED TO SEWN BOOK.

Sewn book. FOLDED SIGNATURES ARE SEWN TOGETHER WITH STRONG THREAD. THIS IS THE MOST COMMON FORM OF BOOKBINDING.

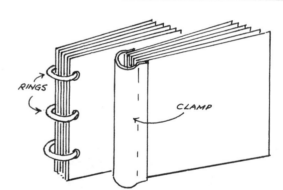

RINGS   CLAMP

Looseleaf binding. PAGES AND COVERS ARE FASTENED TOGETHER WITH CLAMPS OR METAL RINGS.

Other mechanical processes applied to the forms of printed matter are folding, scoring, perforating, diecutting, punching, trimming, embossing, blind stamping, round cornering, drilling, gumming, varnishing, lacquering, and thermography (applying heat to raise the ink). All processes require separate machines and extra costs. Every graphic designer should be completely oriented in them.

Envelopes and mailers

The graphic designer should know the standard envelope forms. If your designed layout is to be mailed, it must fit an envelope, so the design may be affected by the way in which it will be mailed.

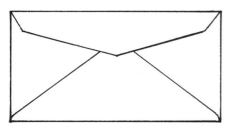

Commercial open side — flap can be sealed (1st class) or tucked in (3rd class)

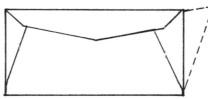

Postage-saver flap can be sealed or unsealed. One end (dotted line) unsealed is 3rd class.

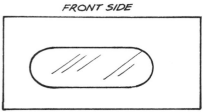

Window — used for statements and invoices.

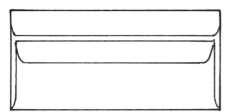

Self-sealing — a time-saver in handling. The flaps have adhesive for instant pressure seal.

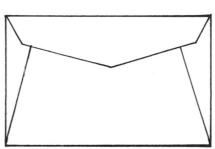

Booklet — open side for direct mail and house organs.

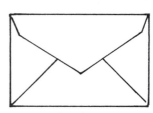

Baronial — fomal deep pointed flap. For invitations, greeting cards, announcements.

SEAL

Self-mailer with seal — does not need an envelope.

LABEL

Mailing tube — ends are sealed or unsealed.

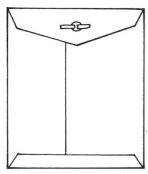

Clasp envelope — flap is closed with metal clasp.

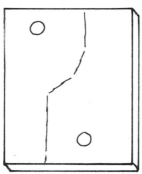

Mailing carton or *expansion envelope.*

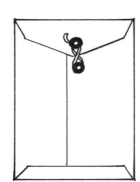

String and button envelope.

BOTH OF THE ABOVE ENVELOPES ARE FOR BULKY ITEMS

219

Handling Art Work

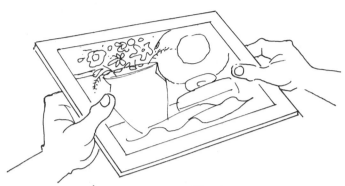

Keep thumbs off the art work.

Always hold the art by the sides, as shown.

Never talk, cough, or sneeze over art, especially when the art is flat, airbrushed and unflapped. Drink your coffee, tea, or anything else, away from the art.

How to minimize loss of your art work.

On the back of every piece of art work (photographs, drawings, and other art) that belongs to you should be your complete name and address. This will minimize any chance of losing the art in transit to the printer, or wherever it is going. A rubber stamp may save you time.

How to keep art you are working on clean

Always rest your hand on a piece of card, or a blotter, when you are working on finished art. Use the left hand to hold the blotter in place. Be careful not to move the card over wet art work.

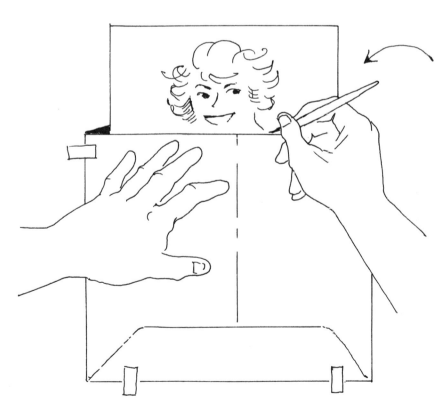

Cut the top from and tape a large clean envelope to your drawing board and put the drawing inside. The drawing has already been sketched out and you are now going to apply the ink or other medium. Slip the sketch out as you proceed with the inking. Your hand will rest on the envelope and the drawing will stay clean. You can make your own envelope with thin cards and tape.

Why you should never prepare tools over artwork

When you sharpen pencil points or fill pens with ink, don't do it over your drawing board, especially if the board has artwork on it. You may accidentally mess up the art with droppings.

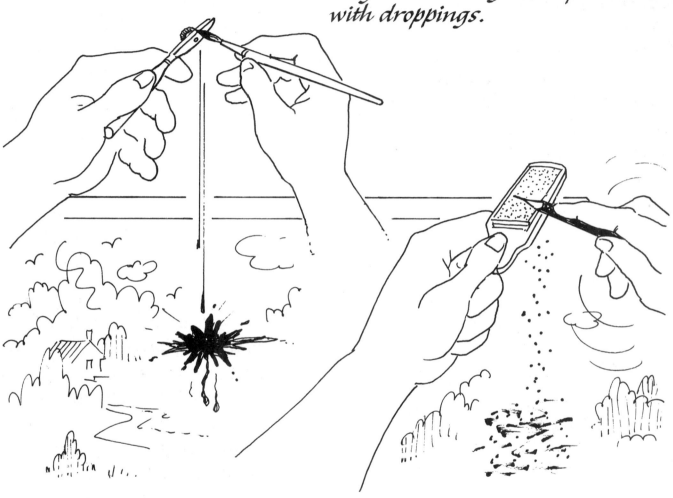

Always do this kind of activity
away from your drawing board.
A good place is over a trash basket.

How to keep clean hands in messy situations

If it is necessary to use your hands in messy situations — as in silk-screen printing, when rubber gloves are not used — first wash your hands in warm water with soap that will give lots of suds. Remove your hands with suds from the water, and rub the hands together until all suds disappear. Dry rub the suds into your hands. Then scratch the soap bar with your fingernails, getting some soap under the nails, and proceed to work. When you are finished and wash your hands in warm water you will find they become clean easily — and under the fingernails, too.

How to prevent things from sticking to your hands in hot weather

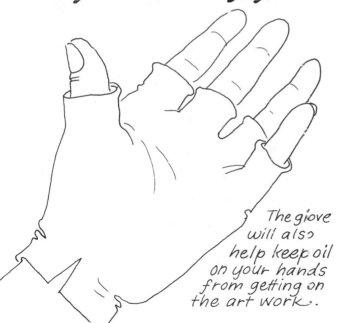

The glove will also help keep oil on your hands from getting on the art work.

If you have a problem due to excessively sweaty hands and hot, humid working conditions, purchase a pair of white cotton gloves (undertaker's gloves are good) and cut the fingers off the glove. Wearing the remaining glove part will eliminate this problem. The glove will not interfere with the normal movement of your fingers.

How to clean up lines in a black-ink drawing

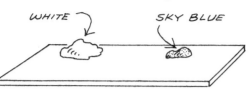

WHITE   SKY BLUE

WATER

MIXING PALLETTE

If you mix a little blue water-color with your opaque white touch-up, it will make your touch-up / clean-up / retouching of ink line art much easier because you will be able to see it. And the light blue will be so light that it will not reproduce when you send the line art to the printer or the engraver.

How to use the back of your hand as a paperweight

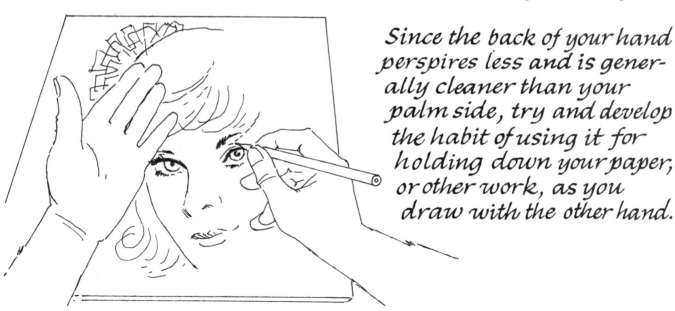

Since the back of your hand perspires less and is generally cleaner than your palm side, try and develop the habit of using it for holding down your paper, or other work, as you draw with the other hand.

How rubber cement can keep a drawing clean

Sometimes, when you are drawing on a board, you will want to keep one special area as clean as possible.

Rubber cement can be used for this purpose. Coat the area you're concerned about with it.

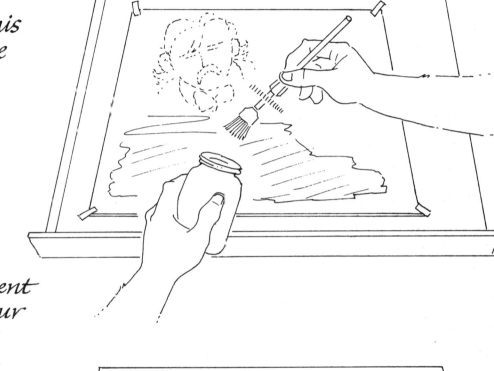

When the cement is dry, make your drawing in the area not covered by the rubber cement and when that part is dry and finished, remove the rubber cement with a pick-up.
You will find that the area is perfectly clean.

How to clean rubber-cement stains from mats

Suppose that you are matting pictures or anything else with rubber cement and you have just finished the first one. It's beautiful—except that you accidentally stained the mat with rubber cement. You clean it with a rag and thinner, but the stain is still there. Here is what you do

1 This is the "finished" stained mat. You may want to remove the picture before proceeding.

2 Spread rubber cement carefully over the entire mat. Do not miss any of the surface, especially the stained areas.

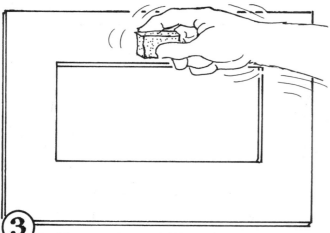

3 When the rubber cement is dry, remove it with a pickup

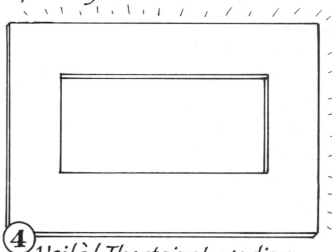

4 Voilà! The stains have disappeared. This method can, of course, be used in similar situations.

How to prevent rubber cement stains on silk-screened paper

If you have many items to adhere to a colored silk screened paper, brush rubber cement over the entire area of the screened paper. After it dries and the items are dry-mounted down, the cement can be picked-

up, leaving no visible stain marks. But if you "spot-cement," the excess cement beyond the limits of the images may leave a stain. The 3 steps below show how to avoid this.

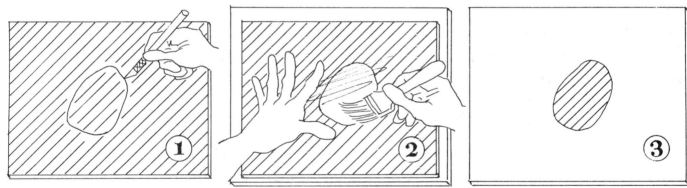

First cut out the shape to be adhered to the screened paper ①. Save the paper left over and use it as a mask to be positioned on the screened paper exactly where you want it ②. Holding the mask against the screened paper, carefully brush rubber cement into the open area ②. Be sure that no rubber cement creeps under the edges. Hold the mask in position until the cement is dry and then remove it. Rubber cement the back of the shape and when it is dry, carefully match its edges with the edges of the rubber cemented area on the screened paper and press. There should be no stains ③.

How to remove graphic-art stains from fabrics

A few methods of removing stains are shown below. If there is a question as to what to do, call an expert dry cleaner immediately. These suggestions may help in the meantime.

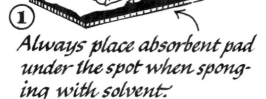

① Always place absorbent pad under the spot when sponging with solvent.

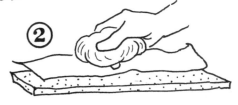

② Sponge with solvent with the spot side down over cloth or blotter.

④ Pour boiling water from a height of about 12" over fabric stretched over a bowl.

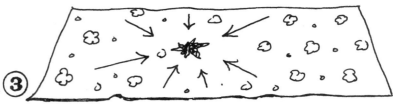

③ Always work from outside in to the center of the spot or stain.

⑤ Always test your reagent on an inconspicuous part of the fabric.

⑥ Never use highly flammable materials such as gasoline or benzene. Friction from rubbing can generate a spark.

⑦ Always rinse all fabrics to remove the reagent.

⑧ Nonflammable solvents (carbon tetrachloride) can be used but they are poisonous, so work in a well-ventilated room, use small quantities, and keep the bottle stoppered while working with it.

⑨ There are 3 kinds of reagents: ① ABSORBENT (cornmeal, dry starch), ② SOLVENTS (water, alcohol, carbon "tet"), and ③ BLEACHES (chlorine, acetic acid solution, white vinegar).

The chart on the following page shows when to use each one.

The chart below shows how to remove different art stains from washable and nonwashable fabrics.

KIND OF STAIN	WASHABLE FABRICS	NONWASHABLE FABRICS
Wax	Scrape off excess with dull knife. Put stained area between 2 blotters and iron with warm iron. If stain remains, sponge with carbon tet or alcohol.	Same as Washable
Dyes	If fabric is white and can be boiled, use commercial color remover (drug store) or bleach with chlorine bleach or hydrogen peroxide. Use bowl or pad method.	Take to expert dry cleaner immediately
Glue	Soak in warm water and launder. If dried, sponge with dilute acetic acid and launder.	Sponge with Carbon tet
Indelible Pencil	Soak in alcohol and launder. If stain remains use chlorine bleach with bowl or pad method.	Take to expert dry cleaner
Ink	While still moist spread with absorbent (cornstarch), brush off and repeat. Launder in warm soap suds. Use commercial ink remover. Soak 1 or 2 days in milk and launder.	Blot up excess and Take to expert dry cleaner
Watercolor Paint	Wash in warm suds	Sponge with carbon tet or turpentine
Oil Paint or Varnish	Sponge with alcohol or carbon tetrachloride.	
Shellac	Soak in equal parts of alcohol and water.	
Alcohol Paints or Stains	Wash in warm suds if fresh or sponge with alcohol. If not fresh, saturate with turpentine and roll up until paint softens. Sponge with more turpentine and launder.	
Wine	Stretch on bowl and cover stain with salt in hot water.	Take to expert dry cleaner
Acrylic Paint	Soak in alcohol and launder	

229

How to use strips of blotters for "mopping up"

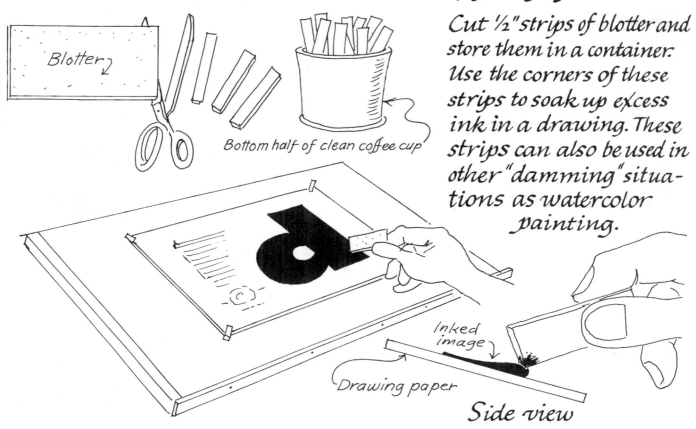

Blotter

Bottom half of clean coffee cup

Inked image

Drawing paper

Side view

Cut ½" strips of blotter and store them in a container. Use the corners of these strips to soak up excess ink in a drawing. These strips can also be used in other "damming" situations as watercolor painting.

How to keep a water jar clean

It's a good idea to add a few drops of a mild detergent to your water jar whenever you change the water. It will not affect the use of the water in most cases, but it will enable you to keep a clean jar, and also make the cleaning of the jar much easier.

Why a blotter should not be used on wet inked lines in art

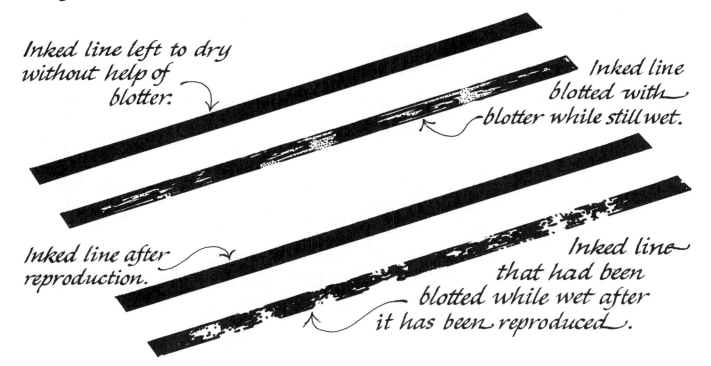

Inked line left to dry without help of blotter.

Inked line blotted with blotter while still wet.

Inked line after reproduction.

Inked line that had been blotted while wet after it has been reproduced.

The demonstration above shows one reason why you should never blot ink lines that will be used for reproduction. If pencil lines have been used to sketch out your drawing first, then inked, dried with a blotter, and erased, the gray of the blotted line will become even weaker. So let your ink lines dry on their own and you will have much happier results in your line-art reproductions. This is particularly true of artwork that uses mainly thin lines, as in crosshatching.

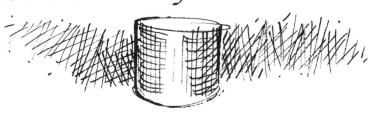

So don't use a blotter. You might also get fuzzy lines or edges that are not sharp and clean.

How to mount clippings and stretch watercolor paper

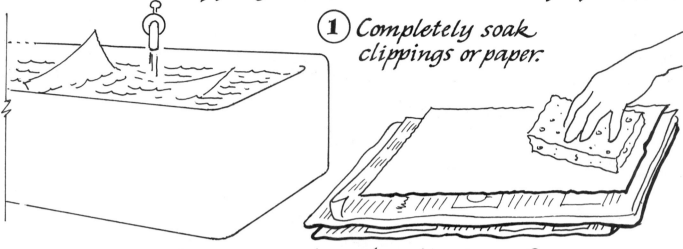

① Completely soak clippings or paper.

② Lay the clippings, face up, on a few newspapers to blot. With a sponge damp dry about 1" around the edges.

GLUE

③ Apply glue with a brush about 1" in from the edges.

PAPER

④ Turn paper over and press onto board. Secure it around the edges with paper tape. Staples can be tacked around the edges. The paper will stretch taut when dry.

5 ways to flatten a curled print

A curled print is carefully uncurled in the direction opposite the curl on a cardboard tube, fastened at the ends with tape, and left for a few days.

 1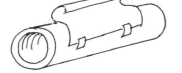

2 If the print is nonglossy the back of the print can be worked back and forth against a smooth corner.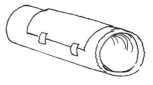

3  First soak the print, if it is unretouched, in water for 5 or 10 minutes. Then hang the wet print on a clothesline and weight it at the bottom.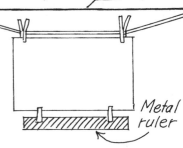

Metal ruler

4 Print 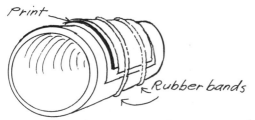 Rubber bands

You can wrap thin cards around the print and then wrap it on a cardboard tube as in ① above. This method is for extremely fragile prints.

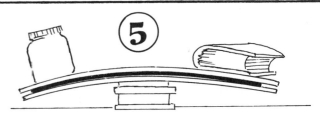 **5**

The print can be inserted between cards, as shown, and bent in the opposite direction of the curl by weights on both sides.

How to make your own portfolio

Expensive leather portfolios are impressive, but what counts most is what is inside. You can make your own portfolio for a modest sum and it will do the job. Neatness and cleanliness, of course, count, and you should keep this in mind.

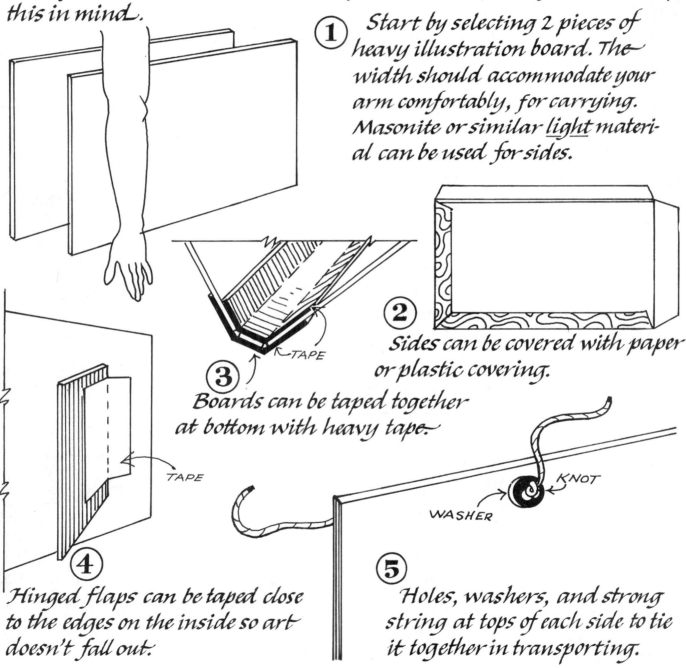

① Start by selecting 2 pieces of heavy illustration board. The width should accommodate your arm comfortably, for carrying. Masonite or similar _light_ material can be used for sides.

② Sides can be covered with paper or plastic covering.

③ Boards can be taped together at bottom with heavy tape.

TAPE

④ Hinged flaps can be taped close to the edges on the inside so art doesn't fall out.

⑤ Holes, washers, and strong string at tops of each side to tie it together in transporting.

KNOT
WASHER

How to mail art work

Lay 2 oversized pieces of corrugated boards (bigger than the art work) over the art, as shown. The corrugated boards are at right angles to each other to minimize the possibility of your package getting bent. Wrap well and put addresses on <u>both</u> sides of the package. Insure and send.

For extra insurance against bending, you can double the pieces, always at right angles to each other.

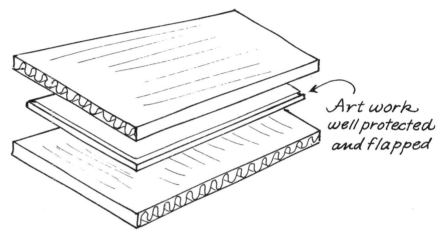

Art work well protected and flapped

Never lay anything on top of flat art work

even if it does have a flap to protect it.

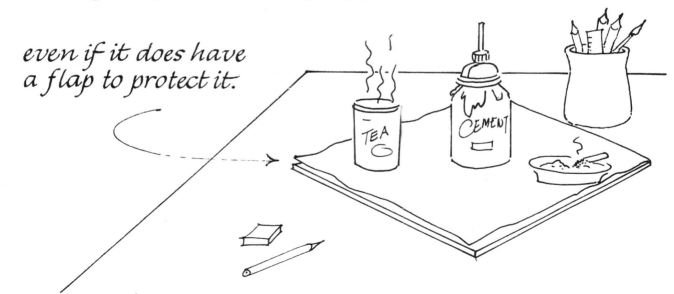

How to mail or transport a drawing or photo

Never fold or roll a drawing or photo—especially one that is to be reproduced by some printing process. This is especially true if you are going to mail it. If you are mailing it, support the art with cardboard stiffeners and supports, with the art sandwiched in between. The art may crack off, especially if retouched, if you roll it, and fold marks on photos will surely reproduce.

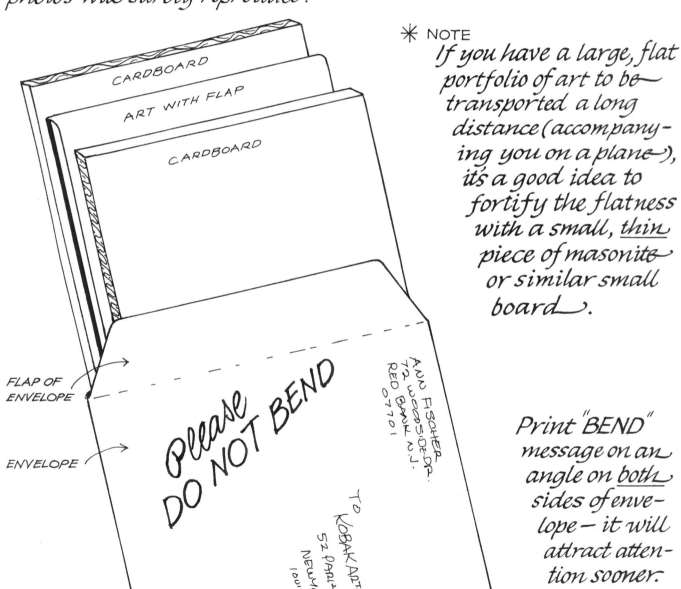

CARDBOARD

ART WITH FLAP

CARDBOARD

FLAP OF
ENVELOPE

ENVELOPE

Please
DO NOT BEND

ANN FISCHER
72 WOODSIDE DR.
RED BANK N.J.
07701

TO
KOBAK ART
52 PARK +
NEW YK
10011

✳ NOTE

If you have a large, flat portfolio of art to be transported a long distance (accompanying you on a plane), it's a good idea to fortify the flatness with a small, <u>thin</u> piece of masonite or similar small board.

Print "BEND" message on an angle on <u>both</u> sides of envelope—it will attract attention sooner.

236

How to make a good mat

The proportions for the width of the mat – from all sides to the hole for the picture – is a matter of personal choice. Most artists will agree to the points expressed below on making a good mat, even though there are always the exceptions, for various effects. to these "rules." First let's look at bad mats.

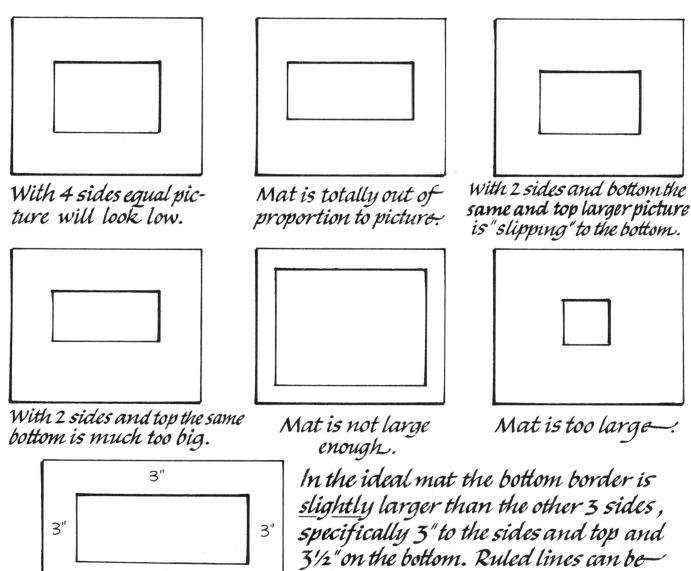

With 4 sides equal picture will look low.

Mat is totally out of proportion to picture.

With 2 sides and bottom the same and top larger picture is "slipping" to the bottom.

With 2 sides and top the same bottom is much too big.

Mat is not large enough.

Mat is too large.

In the ideal mat the bottom border is _slightly_ larger than the other 3 sides, specifically 3" to the sides and top and 3½" on the bottom. Ruled lines can be added.

How to clean a mat

There may be an occasion when you want to clean a soiled mat. First lay the mat flat on a clean level surface. Dust with a clean cloth or a brush to remove all loose particles and then rub it with a soft kneaded eraser. An abrasive ink eraser, used gently, and sharp stencil knives and eraser may remove stubborn spots, but you must be careful never to damage the surface. Also try clean rags and rubber cement thinner, gently rubbed over and over the mat. Finally, if necessary, use lacquer thinner with cotton balls, to clean the mat completely.

Cleaning agents →

INK ERASER

RUBBER CEMENT THINNERS

LACQUER THINNER

KNEADED ERASER

COTTON BALLS

Q-TIP

How to clean off stubborn rubber cement smudges

Any one, or all, of the above suggestions for cleaning a mat can also be used to clean stubborn smudges from a completed mechanical. Try not to damage the surface, but if you do, dab light touches of white retouch paint to the scuffed areas with the aid of a cotton ball or a small piece of sponge. The mechanical, too, should lie flat on a clean level surface.

WHITE

Frames
How to repair old picture frames

An old picture frame can be cleaned and refinished with a few repair ideas, shown below, perhaps saving you the cost of a new one.

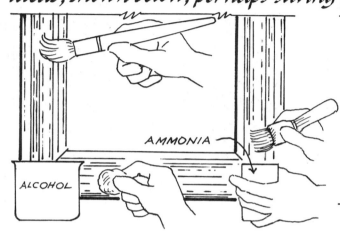

First dry-clean the frame with gentle strokes of a small bristle brush. Then dip cotton into denatured alcohol and gently rub the frame to remove caked-on dirt. Do not rub hard. If the frame is covered with gold leaf or gold paint, apply ammonia and water with a soft brush and blot dry. Do not rub.

Small scratches on gold frames can be rubbed with a matching gold wax-based paste using a small folded cloth.

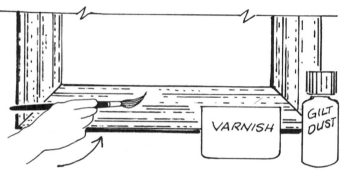

Clean the scratch marks, apply varnish, and, when tacky-dry, pat on gilt powder. When dry the next day, lightly buff the area with clean cotton.

In cleaning a palette knife, toothpick, or smooth sandpaper can help the job, but do not overdo the rubbing. Steel wool and your finger are other "tools."

Scratches on other finished frames besides gold can be touched up with sticks or stains that match. Ornate frames can be built up with gesso, vinyl, or acrylic speckling paste, which you can buy in paint or hardware stores.

ow to plan picture and frame sizes

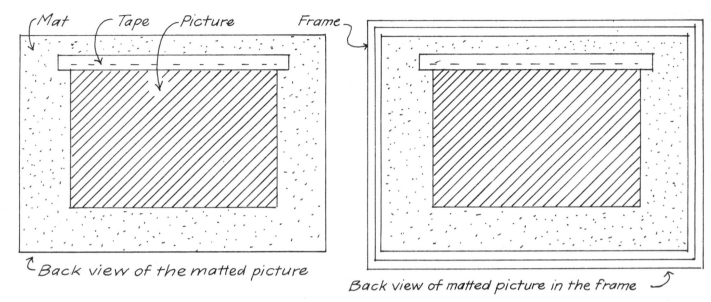

Mat   Tape   Picture   Frame

Back view of the matted picture

Back view of matted picture in the frame

When frame sizes are given, the size refers to the matted picture which fits the back of the frame, not the actual size of the frame. Standard frame (picture) sizes are listed below. Special frames can be made to order:

5" × 7"	8" × 10"	9" × 12"	10" × 14"
11" × 14"	12" × 16"	14" × 18"	16" × 20"
18" × 24"	20" × 24"	22" × 28"	24" × 30"
24" × 36"			

Until you have the facilities for making your own frames, it would be well to limit your framable pictures to these sizes.

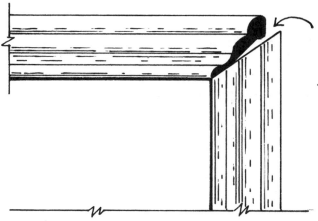

If frame is warped and corners become separated, clean the joints, sandpaper, and glue together.

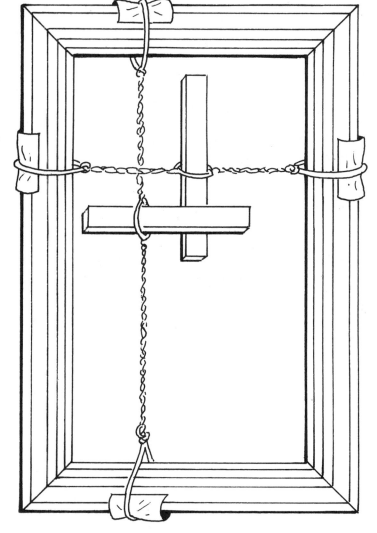

Wrap strong twine around frame (near joints) as shown here.

"Tourneguet" with small pieces of wood but do not pull, or bow, the sides of the frame. Protect the frame edges with folded cards.

On simple fractures clean as best you can and apply glue and tournequets, patching with plastic wood if necessary. When dry rub with fine sandpaper. Then apply finish and buff with a soft rag.

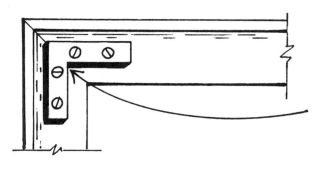

Flat angle irons can be screwed into the back corners if the frame has flat sides on the back. Angle in the screws to pull the pieces of frame together.

Formulas

Here are some formulas for circular forms and a pyramid.

 Circumference of circle is the diameter times pi (π). Pi is 3.14159265 or 3.1416.

 Area of circle = diameter x 0.7854, or πr^2.

 Area of sphere (surface) = (radius² x 3.1416) x 4.

Volume of sphere = [(radius x radius x radius x π) x 4] ÷ 3.

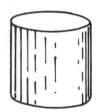 Area of cylinder = circumference of top (or base) x height plus areas of top and base.

Volume of cylinder = (radius² x π) x height.

 Area of cone = (slant height x circumference) ÷ 2 + area of base.

Volume of cone = (altitude x area of base) ÷ 3.

Area of pyramid = (slant height x perimeter of base) ÷ 2 + area of base.

Volume of pyramid = (altitude x area of base) ÷ 3.

WATCH WHERE THOSE DECIMAL POINTS GO!

Circle Formulas
How to find parts of circles and globes

All circles
have 360°

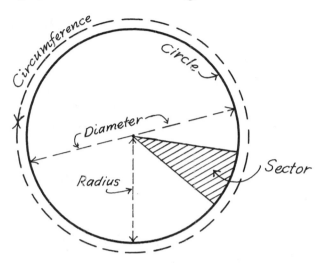

Formulas

To find the <u>diameter</u> of a circle, multiply the circumference by .31831

To find the <u>circumference</u> of a circle, multiply the diameter by 3.1416

To find the <u>area</u> of a circle, multiply the square of the diameter by .7854

To find the <u>surface</u> of a ball, multiply the square of the diameter by 3.1416

Suppose you have a circle and a square both of which have the same known area. You want to know the length of a side of the square. You find this by dividing the area of either the circle or the square by .8862.

To find the <u>cubic volume</u> in a ball, multiply the cube of the diameter by .5236
The cube is the diameter x the diameter x the diameter.

To find the <u>area</u> of a <u>sector</u>, use the following formula:

$$\text{Area of sector} = \frac{\substack{\text{angle of the sides} \\ \text{of the sector (radii)}}}{360} \; X \; \text{the area of the circle}$$

Note where the decimal points are in each case shown above.

Metric Equivalents for Easy Reference

Linear Measures

1 centimeter	0.3937 inch
1 inch	2.54 centimeters
1 decimeter	3.937 inches, 0.328 foot
1 foot	3.048 decimeters
1 meter	39.37 inches, 1.09.36 yards
1 yard	0.9144 meter
1 decameter	1.9884 rods
1 rod	0.5029 decameter
1 kilometer	0.621.37 mile
1 mile	1.609.3 kilometers

Square Measures

1 sq. centimeter	0.1550 sq. inch
1 sq. inch	6.452 sq. centimeters
1 sq. decimeter	0.1076 sq. foot
1 sq. foot	9.2903 sq. decimeters
1 sq. meter	1.196 sq. yards
1 sq. yard	0.8361 sq. meter
1 acre	160 sq. rods
1 sq. rod	0.00625 acre
1 hectare	2.47 acres
1 acre	0.4047 hectare
1 sq. kilometer	0.386 sq. mile
1 sq. mile	2.59 sq. kilometers

Measures of Volume

1 cu. centimeter	0.061 cu. inch
1 cu. inch	16.39 cu. centimeters
1 cu. decimeter	0.0353 cu. foot
1 cu. foot	28.317 cu. decimeters
1 cu. yard	0.7646 cu. meter
1 stere	0.2759 cord
1 cord	3.624 steres
1 liter	0.908 qt. dry, 1.0567 qts. liq.
1 qt. dry	1.101 liters
1 qt. liquid	0.9463 liter
1 decaliter	2.6417 gals., 1.135 pecks
1 gal.	0.3785 decaliter
1 peck	0.881 decaliter
1 hectoliter	2.8375 bushels
1 bushel	0.3524 hectoliter

Weights

1 gram	0.03527 ounce
1 ounce	28.35 grams
1 kilogram	2.2046 pounds
1 pound	0.4536 kilogram
1 metric ton	0.98421 English ton
1 English ton	1.016 metric tons

Get an education from reading art dealers' catalogs

Reading good art dealers' catalogs is a splendid way to obtain not only all kinds of information about the tools of the craft but also a complete orientation as to what supplies are available. You may be surprised to find that that thing you saw in a studio is for making ellipses, for example. Many good catalogs are full of informative material such as where the hair for the best artists' brushes comes from.

And they are free!!
(IN MOST PLACES)

Business
Tips on getting a job

The following items are listed in no particular order, but all are signicant in getting a job, whether it's your first or fiftieth.

1. Make sure that you have an appointment and don't be late. Don't ever come to an art office cold without being expected.

2. Have a clean portfolio – it doesn't have to be an expensive one. You will not get a job on the leather but what's inside.

3. Put into your portfolio your best work only, even though it may be only a few pieces.

4. If you are showing watercolors or prints, mat them.

5. Keep pieces relatively the same size. If this is not possible, mat the smaller pieces or put two or more small ones on one mat.

6. Neatness and cleanliness count for your art as well as for yourself.

7. If you have worked before, have an extra resumé to leave. Your resumé should show address, schools, prizes, interests, photo of yourself, etc.

8. If you have 3-dimensional material, have photos of it to show.

9. Be pleasant. No-one wants to work with a sourpuss. Don't oversell yourself. Talk little – not excessively or loudly.

10. Never borrow someone else's art to show as your own.

11. Don't say that copied art is original. "They" know.

12. Don't repeat too much of the same thing. Show variety if possible. Portfolios get to be heavy with an excess of similar pieces.

13. If you don't get a job leave in a pleasant way, thanking "them" for their time. They may need you in a few months.

246

How to run a small art service in your own home

A young artist with talent and enthusiasm can start a small art service at home. If equipment such as a copier machine, multigraph machine, typewriter, and photostat machine is available, it will make your work much easier. Samples of your art that relate to what prospective clients can use and samples of work that you have done for others should be included in a portfolio to show new customers. An example of what you can do is shown below.

YOUR ART

The layout above will never win an art director's award. It is shown as a simple example of what a resourceful artist can do. Stencils for typewritten matter can be positioned and "cut" on a typewriter. Other elements can be silkscreened or photostated after manipulation and positioned on the master paste-up. Final copies can be printed in quantity on the copier before silkscreening.

You can make your own silkscreens for display art in color after printing all the copies on copier.

Transfer lettering sheets, all styles, can be composed and photostated larger or smaller to fit your layout.

Index